T0064060

PROPHETS
—AND—
PROPHETIC
MINISTRY

PROPHETS —AND— PROPHETIC
MINISTRY

M. Victor Sagayaraj

PARTRIDGE

To order additional copies of this book, contact
Partridge India
000 800 10062 62
orders.india@partridgepublishing.com

www.partridgepublishing.com/india

CONTENTS

FOREWORD

The much abused gift today is "Prophetic Gift". Everybody in this world wants to know what the future holds for him / her, forgetting the one who holds the future. Being an Asian, I can say that the eastern culture is very much interknitted with divination and thus this gift has become very commercial too.

Among God's people also it is visible. Some elected are also deceived to the extend of ignoring the warning note of the Holy Scripture. It may be because of their inclination of having "itching ears". The Bible warns us that "my people perish because of lack of knowledge"(Hosea:4:6).

Again the office of the prophet is also a greatly misunderstood subject today. If it is realised fully, along with an apostle the prophet can shake the walls of the prison(Acts:16:25,26) and lay new foundation of freedom for the captives.To have a clear Biblical understanding we need to see everything in the light of the revealed inspired scriptures. Bro. Victor Sagayaraj brought out a beautiful well defined book on this subject. I praise God for his work which will definitely bring clarity in the hearts and minds of people.

It is my prayer that his work may bring an impact upon the Church of God at this needy hour. May the Lord's anointing help him to write more books which can reform and re-educate the Church to unlearn the unwanted things which have crept into God's Church.

D.Augustine Jebakumar,
General Secretary,
Gospel Echoing Missionary Society, Bihar, India

A Few Comments From The Readers:

Prophecy is one of the most misunderstood and misinterpreted subjects of the Bible. Among evangelical Christians this is a much desired gift, but for all the wrong reasons. I appreciate Bro. Victor Sagayaraj's insight into this subject, and I believe he has brought out the Biblical perspective correctly and thoroughly in this book.

Prophecy is a spiritual gift meant to reveal hidden secrets of the past, present and future to warn, guide, and equip the children of God to be effective in God's purposes. Biblical prophecy reveals God's plan through the ages, and connects them to the first and second coming of Jesus Christ. Properly exercised, prophecy can bring cleansing, reverence, and edification in the body of Christ.

I pray that every reader of this book may be gifted with this insight, so that God can use them and bless them for such a time as this. May the Lord continue to bless Brother Victor and his family for the furtherance of the Gospel.

Pastor Kunju Raju, New York

Kings, priests and prophets are the 3 anointed offices in the Bible. Powerful kings and dignified priests lived royally; but the life of a prophet is not a bed of roses, but of thorns.

Prophets, with no significant address in the society, shook the entire world. They placed Kings on the throne as well as dethroned them. As a mouthpiece of God, they heralded His burden to the kings and common people. Horses and chariots of fire were their security.

The Author served the Indian Air Force for 2 decades and has got a divine revelation on this subject. This book unequivocally is packed with the expounded teaching on Prophets and their ministry. I hope that this book will be a great blessing to today's Christendom.

E.L. Ephraim, M.com, M.Phil, M.A, M.Ed,
Managing Trustee, Blessing Ministries, India

This book provides the reader a clear and systematic study on the ministry of prophets found in the New and Old testaments. The content is theologically balanced and Scripturally sound and a very valuable resource for both leaders and laity. The author touches on all aspects related to this very sensitive and relevant topic in a very erudite way. A very timely book for the end time Church at large.

Cherian John, Senior Pastor, Faith Community Centre, Chandigarh, India

PREFACE

Grace be unto you and peace from God our Father and the Lord Jesus Christ. I hope these messages will be of great help to hold fast the most holy faith, which is once committed to the saints. Apostle Paul warned the Church saying, "But know this, that in the last days perilous times will come." (2 Timothy 3:1-3) Eventually, those who have the spiritual insight can understand clearly that we're living right now in such a time.

What's happening in the present day Church? Many abominable things crept into the Temple of God and defiled it as it was so in the days of Ezekiel. People embrace **another Gospel** -- leaving the true Gospel of God, seek **another Christ** -- rejecting the Crucified Christ, and follow **another spirit** – neglecting the Spirit of truth. The people of God go astray from the original track of faith because of lack of knowledge, lack of discernment, and lack of vigilance. When will we identify the strange fire which is burning inside the *cold churches?*

But, at this adverse and darkness encapsulated environment, the Spirit of God -- like a mighty wind -- is going to cause a great prophetic move in the Body of Christ. And this move will ultimately pave the way for **a great Revival, a wholesome Restoration, and a final Reformation** in His Body. It's time for diligent seekers of God to understand the heavy burden, the deeper heart-cry, and the persistent travailing of the Holy Spirit. Need of this hour is for a trumpet blowing prophetic team to express the mind of God.

I thank God for the grace, the revelations, and the guidance He gave me to write this book. I thank my beloved wife Jeyanthi who has been a great encouragement in writing this book. I thank my dear sons, Paul Finney and Jeremy Titus, for their fervent encouragement in this work. I'm thankful to Missionary Chinna Thambi, Blessing youth Mission, who helped me a lot to compose this book initially in Tamil. I'm also thankful to Sister Krishnabai Charles, who assisted me sincerely in translating them into English.

I pray that, in the forthcoming Revival, God may mightily use everyone who reads this book. May the blessings of the Lord rest upon you.

Your fellow labourer in Christ,
Bro. Victor Sagayaraj
Vicjey2011@gmail.com

CHAPTER 1

Present Day Prophets

1.1 Does God send his prophets in
this present time?

Does God send his prophets presently? The Bible affirms that prophets are necessary for the edification of the Church, to prepare the people of God for the ministry and for the perfection of the Church.

"And He Himself gave some to be apostles, some PROPHETS, some evangelists, and some pastors and teachers, for the equipping of the saints for the work of the ministry, for the edifying of the Body of Christ, till we all come to the unity of the faith and of the knowledge of the Son of God, to a perfect man, to the measure of the stature of the fullness of Christ." (Eph. 4:11-13)

There is a difference between the ministries of the New Testament prophets and the Old Testament prophets. Knowledge about the prophets is necessary for believers to understand the New Testament prophetic ministry rightly, and to identify false prophets. Prophets are not confined to a single local church. Though they are members of a specific local church, they have ministry outside the local church also. Agabus, Silas and Judas were prophets of the local church in Jerusalem, but they did their prophetic ministry in other places too like Antioch and Caesria.

(Eph. 4:11, 1 Cor. 12:28, Acts 11:27, 28; 21:8-11; 15:22, 30,32)

1.2 Meaning of Prophets

Prophets were earlier known as **"seers"** because their eyes were opened and they saw visions from God. They were also called **watchmen, servants, shepherds, messengers of God, men of God, ministers of God and visionaries.**

God revealed them future events and the corrupted state of His people. Prophets are the spokesmen of God. They are separated even from their mothers' wombs to live for God. They are sent by God to give the current message of God. During the Old Testament days God raised up His prophets again and again to declare His **"current word"** to His people so that they might turn from their evil ways. The wicked also declared the future events. Prophets directly speak the word of God to the people of their generation.

Prophets are sent by God. John the Baptist was sent by God as his messenger to prepare the way for the ministry of the Lord Jesus Christ. We know that how God sent Moses to Egypt. Prophets like Isaiah and Jeremiah declared with assurance that they were sent by God to prophesy. They are not supposed to go to anyone as per their wish. The Bible speaks about the prophets of four ages. Firstly, the prophets of the Old Covenant – till John the Baptist. Secondly, the inter-testament prophet—Lord Jesus Christ. Thirdly, New Testament prophets of the Church age (prophets after the resurrection of Christ or present day prophets). Fourthly, the tribulation prophets who would do the prophetic ministry during the tribulation period.

(1 Sam. 9:9, Amos 7:12, Isa. 29:10, Num.24:3, 4, Ezek.3:17, Jer. 6:17, Zech. 11:5,6, Hag. 1:13, Deut. 33:1, 1Sam. 2:27, II Kings. 4:9, 21:10, Isa. 30:10, Luke 7:27, Isa. 48:16, Jer.26:12, Matt. 11:13, Deut 18:15, 1Cor. 12:28, Rev.11:3-6)

1.3 The New Testament Prophets

Ephesians 4:11 certainly speaks about the New Testament Prophets and Jesus Christ is still giving Prophets to the New Testament Church as gifts. According to the Scripture, when Christ ascended on high, He led captivity captive, and gave gifts to men and which he will continue to do till the Church becomes a perfect man with the measure of the stature of the fullness of Christ. Furthermore, Apostle Paul assures in the book of Corinthians that only a few people function in the office of the Prophets.

Let us see some of the New Testament prophets from the Bible:-

➢ Judas, Agabus and Silas were prophets in the Jerusalem church.

3

- ➤ Barnabas, Simeon, Lucius, Manaen and Saul (Apostle Paul) were prophets and teachers in the church at Antioch.
- ➤ Prophets (whose names are not given) sent from Jerusalem to Antioch.
- ➤ There were prophets in Corinth church.
- ➤ The prophetic office of Apostle John, the writer of the Book of Revelation, is confirmed by his prophetic visions and (prophetic) revelations he received at Patmos.

Prophetic ministry is quite ancient and has been existing for a longer period. God Himself uttered the first prophecy in Eden. Enoch prophesied about the second coming of Christ. God will continue to send his prophets till the time of tribulation.

(Eph4: 8-13, 1Cor.12:29, Act. 15:32, 13:1, 11:27, 28, 1Cor. 14:29, Gen. 3:15, Rev. 1:1-3, 10: 9, 10)

CHAPTER 2

Ministry of the New Testament Prophets

2.1 They build up the church

It's an undeniable fact that the New Testament Church is being built upon the foundation of the Apostles and Prophets. Ministry of the prophets is necessary for the believers and for the ministers in the churches as they play an important role in building up of the Church. Before Silas was commissioned for the apostolic ministry, along with Judas, he exhorted the brethren as a prophet. Anyone who prophesies ultimately edifies, exhorts, and comforts the church. Along with the other four ministries, they play a major role in building up the church. Ministry of the prophets is necessary for us to grow up in **all things into Jesus Christ, the head.**

(1Pet. 1:10, Eph.2:20, Act.15:32, 1Cor.14:3, 4, Eph.4: 11,15, Rom. 12:10, Act. 15:31, 32)

M. Victor Sagayaraj

2.2 They confirm the will of God

In the Old Testament days, God revealed His will to the people through the prophets. In the New Testament days, God's will is made known to the believers through the indwelling Holy Spirit. It can be confirmed by the prophets of the New Testament. When Paul and Barnabas stayed on in the Antioch church, without fulfilling the ministry for which they had been called, the prophets confirmed the will of God concerning their work, which they have already received.

(Rom. 8:14, Act. 13:2)

2.3 They warn the believers

Warnings concerning the dangers, natural calamities, satanic attacks, and God's judgment are being prophesied. Prophet Agabus warned about the terrible famine that was to come all over the world in the first century. The same prophet also warned Apostle Paul that he would be bound in Jerusalem. In the city of Tyre, Paul was warned by a prophecy -- not to go the Jerusalem. In the book of Revelation, we find that Smyrna church received a prophetic warning about the future tribulation while Thyatira church was warned about the judgment of Jezebel. Prophetic warnings protect God's people from the attacks of the enemy too. Jonah's warning caused a great repentance in the city of Nineveh. Prophets are under the obligation to bring the word of Judgment from God. Ezekiel, as a watchman, was entrusted with the responsibility to warn the people and failure to warn the wicked was considered as a serious offence.

(Act.11:27-30. Act. 21:11, Rev. 2:10, Rev.2:20-23, Jonah 3,1Kings 21:19-24, Ezek 33:7, 8)

2.4 Prophets expose the sins of the people of God

Prophets of the Old Testament exposed the sins of the Israelites and the New Testament Prophets exposed the sins of the local churches. Though Jesus Christ held the elders of the seven churches in His right hand, He exposed the sins of those churches through Prophet John. Through the gift of the word of knowledge, prophets can know the hidden sins of the people. Prophet Nathan revealed the sin of Kind David. John the Baptist exposed the sin of King Herod. Jesus Himself exposed the sin of the Samaritan woman. Prophet Micah was filled with power by the Spirit of the LORD, and of justice, and might, to declare to Jacob his transgression, and to Israel his sin. Paul says that through prophecy the secrets of men can be exposed.

True prophets will never compromise with sin -- they will expose sin as sin. God exposes the sins of His people through his prophets in order to correct them. God also gives wisdom to them to do this work in the appropriate time and in a decent manner. God gives the responsibility to them to declare the sins of the people and the state of their inward spiritual condition directly or indirectly. Pharisees, the highly religious sect of Judaism, were boasting that they were descendants of Abraham, but Jesus did not hesitate to expose their inward spiritual condition by saying, "You are of your father the devil and the desires of your father you want to do."

Mere preaches may help anybody and hurt nobody; but Prophets will stir everybody and madden somebody. The preacher may go with the crowd; but the prophet goes against it. A man freed, fired, and filled with God will be branded unpatriotic because he speaks against his nation's sins; unkind because his tongue is a two-edged sword; unbalanced because the weight of preaching opinion is against him. The preacher will be heralded; the prophet hounded.

--Leonard Ravenhill

(Rev. 1:20, 2 Sam.12:12, Mark 6:17, 18, 1Cor.14:24, 25, 2 Sam. 11& 12, John 4:18, 19, 8:44, Micah 3:8)

2.5 Prophets train others for prophetic ministry

Prophets have to prepare the believers also for prophetic ministry. The Bible affirms that in the days of Prophet Samuel and of Elijah and Elisha there were schools of the prophets. There was a big group of prophets in **Bethel and Jericho.** In those days, sons of the prophets were trained by the senior prophets in many places. At the same time, we must remember that prophets are never made by men, but they are made by God. Samuel took the lead to train a group of prophets during his days. Moses, being a great prophet of the Old Testament, encouraged the prophetic ministry of other elders. Prophet Elijah trained Elisha in prophetic ministry. New Testament churches should be prophetic institutes where mature prophets should train God's people for prophetic ministry.

(Eph.4:11-13, 1Sam.10:10, II Kings 2,3,5,7 chapters, 1Sam.19:20, Num.11:26-30,1Kings19-21chapters)

2.6 Prophets challenge false prophets

True prophets of God contend with false prophets. Jeremiah, Ezekiel, Micah, Amos and Paul challenged the false prophets in their ministries. Elijah challenged 450 prophets of Baal. Micah, Jeremiah, Ezekiel prophesied against false prophets. Paul declared judgment of God upon a false prophet who stood against the Gospel. Obviously, the true prophets will never compromise with the false prophets.

(II Kings 18.22&25, Micah 3: 5 & 6, Jer. 8:10-12, Ezek 13:17-21, Acts 13:6-11)

2.7 They call people unto repentance

Jesus Christ thundered during his preaching that unless the people repent they would perish miserably. It's the ultimate cry of any genuine prophet, "**Repent or you will perish.**" What has happened to the present day prophets? They are willing to please the people more than urging them to repent. Consider what the prophet Paul preached on the Mars' Hill in Athens, "God now commands all men everywhere to repent." My heart yearns for preachers such as Jonathan Edwards, who preached the famous sermon *"Sinners in the hands of an angry God"*.

Some argue that depressed people need comfort while God's command is that all people should repent. **If there is going to be a revival, there must necessarily be the message of repentance.** When God looked for someone whom He could send to preach repentance at the end of the first century. He could find none other than a prophet in the island of Patmos. There was no other way to send the message of repentance to God's people except writing letters with the message of repentance to the local churches. The seven stars that he carefully held in His right hand had failed to preach repentance. The same condition prevails in today's churches. Jesus rebuked the unrepentant cities like Chorazin and Bethsaida. Today, we need Prophets who can preach repentance -- prophets thundering the message of repentance before revival is the history.

(Luke 13:5, Matt. 4:17, Acts17:30, Matt. 11:20-24)

CHAPTER 3

Qualifications of
A True Prophet

God trains and equips his prophets by giving them spiritual gifts and power -- according to His calling -- to do His will in the Church. Without God's calling no one can ever be qualified to be a prophet. The calling of God, prophetic anointing, and the gifts of the Holy Spirit prove a prophet's ministry.

3.1 The calling of a prophet

No one can do the ministry of a prophet without a specific call of God. It came to prophet Isaiah when he was in his mother's womb while prophet Jeremiah, a son of a priest, was ordained by God as a prophet when he was in his mother's womb. During the Babylonian captivity, God called priest Ezekiel to be a prophet and commissioned him to prophesy to the nation Israel. John the Baptist was also a priest by birth and the word of God came to him at the appointed time. He was to serve as a priest in the temple at the age of 30, but served as a prophet according to Zecharia's prophecy. Amos was a herdsman and a tender of sycamore fruit and the Lord called him and made him a prophet. In Patmos, Apostle John was commanded to prophesy.

(Isa. 49:1,2, 5, 48:16, Jer. 1:5, Eze.2:3, 4, Luke 3:2, Amos 7:15, Rev 10:11)

3.2 Prophetic Anointing

Prophetic anointing is a specific anointing and it's impossible to function as a prophet without the anointing. Prophets were referred by God as the **anointed ones.** During their prophetic ministry, this anointing descends upon them again and again. As the Spirit of God fell upon Ezekiel he was urged to prophesy. We can clearly see that the prophetic anointing was upon Moses **and later on the same anointing was taken from him and was placed upon the seventy elders.** Prophetic anointing was also upon Elijah as well as upon Elisha.

(Zech 4:6, 14, Acts 13:9-11, Ezek 11:5, Num.11:25, 1 Kings 19:16)

3.3 Gifts and the Power of the Spirit

In general, prophets have the **gift of prophecy, the word of wisdom, the word of knowledge, and the discerning of the spirits**. These gifts help them to play their role effectively. **Gift of prophecy** denotes speaking from the mind of God with the help of the Holy Spirit. **The word of knowledge** gives revelation beyond the natural -- without the aid of intellectual knowledge -- either about a person or about past, present, and future events.

The word of wisdom is the revelation or utterance that is beyond the natural, given to believers by the Holy Spirit to know, to speak or to act in a particular circumstance. **The gift of discernment of spirits** is the ability beyond the natural to identify rightly the activities of various spirits (The Holy Spirit, the human spirit and the evil spirit). This is not the intellectual discernment based on Biblical knowledge.

In addition to these gifts, some prophets may have the power gifts such as, gift of faith, gift of healings, and working of miracles (Moses, Elijah and Jesus Christ). At the same time, we can also find a few prophets without these power gifts in the Bible. John the Baptist, Agabus, Jude, and Silas also didn't do any miracle. But the two prophets of the tribulation period will have supernatural signs -- like Elijah and Moses – and they would do miracles and wonders. God anointed Jesus of Nazareth with the Holy Spirit and with the power to do great miracles. Elisha experienced the power of God in a twofold measure. Even after his death, God's power was stored in his bones; a few months after his death, a dead man's body touched Elisha's bones, and he became alive.

(John 4:18, 19, II Sam. 21:14, II Kings 5:12, Math. 9:26, Jn. 4:17, 19, Acts 5:1-9, Matt. 22:21, Luke 12:12, Acts 15:13-21, 16:16-18, 10:38, Rev. 11:3-6, II Kings. 13:21)

3.4 Prophet's burden

"My eyes overflow with rivers of water for the destruction of the daughter of my people." "...... but His word was in my

heart like a burning fire shut up in my bones; I was weary of holding it back and I could not." "..My heart makes a noise in me; I cannot hold my peace." (Jer. 20:9, 4:19)

Above verses reveal how Jeremiah lamented and shed tears for the people of Israel. The vision that Habakkuk saw became a burden to him. Malachi declared God's word as the burden of the Lord. Isaiah had the burden for many nations: burden of Babylon, Moab, Damascus, Egypt, wilderness of the Sea, Dumah, Arabia, the valley of vision, and Tyre. Isaiah wanted to weep bitterly for the sake of his people. **Ultimately, the burden of God's heart becomes the burden of a prophet**. God's burden is merged with God's word. As they cannot hold the revealed word of God, God's burden presses them down. Because of the burden of God, they not only shed tears but also burned up with anger and rebuke people.

(Lam. 3:48, Hab. 1:1, Isa.13:1, 15:1, 17:1, 19:1, 21:1, 23:1, 21:1,11,13, 22:4)

3.5 Visions

"If there a prophet among you, I, the LORD, make Myself known to him in a vision…" (Num.12:6)

Prophets receive visions from God. God speaks to them through visions repeatedly. Prophets are basically "**seers**". They not only see visions but also get the interpretations of the visions. All those who see visions are not prophets, but God's prophets do see visions. The visions that they

see get merged with their lives, and they usually stand firm for such visions. Their visions penetrate deeply into their lives and ministries. They consider God's visions as their own and carry them. Apostle Paul had a vision for **a glorious and a holy Church** – without any spot or wrinkle or blemish. John had a vision of the New Jerusalem. Ezekiel was commissioned to declare everything he **saw** concerning the house of Israel.

(Dan. 8:15-17, Zech. 5:1-4, Rev. 17:6, Eph. 5:27, Rev. 21:2, Ezek40:4)

3.6 Dreams

"If there is a prophet among you..... I speak to him in a dream." (Num.12:6)

God mostly reveals the future events to His prophets through dreams. They receive the interpretation too. Joseph and Daniel had the ability to interpret the dreams of other people too. A Prophet, who had a dream, was expected to tell that dream to others. God does not give visions and dreams just for the sake of excitement, but He reveals the things that can't be perceived by natural means.

(Dan. 7:11, 7:16, Gen. 40: 1-23, 41:16-27, Dan. 4:18-26, Jer.23:28-33)

3.7 They receive the word directly

Prophets receive the word (Rhema) directly from God. In fact, God **puts his words in the mouth of his prophets.** They receive some counseling or concepts from God. They receive the very word that is to be made known, directly from God. Perhaps, every prophet has to receive the current words directly from God for his ministry. Prophets receive the word of God through visions or dreams or the word of knowledge or visitation of angels or the inner voice or the Scriptures. They do not always understand the meaning of the word unless God explains them.

(Ezek 7:1 and Luke 3:2, Jer. 1:9, Jer1:4, Ezek 3:1, Rev. 10:10, Dan. 8:1-4, Ezek 34:37, Dan. 7:1, 8:15,16,1Sam. 3:7-14, Jer. 1:9, I Pet. 1:10-12, Dan. 12:8,7:15, 16)

3.8 Revelations regarding God's plans

The sovereign God does nothing without revealing his secrets to his servants -- the prophets. God told Abraham about the destruction of Sodom and Gomorrah. God informed concerning the things that would happen in the future in the heavens and on earth. Though mysteries are revealed to all the believers in the New Testament, deep mysteries are revealed to the prophets through the Holy Spirit. God has a plan for every individual, for His Church, for Israel, and for other countries too. He reveals His plans in the appropriate time to his prophets.

(Amos 3:7, Gen. 18:17-22, 20:17, Rev. 1:1, John 16:13, Eph.3: 3,6)

3.9 Revelations of the Lord's Church

In the first Centaury, the mystery of the Body of Christ, hidden during the previous ages, was revealed to the Apostles and prophets. They have the vision regarding the Universal Body of the Lord Jesus Christ. They also have the knowledge of God's plans regarding His Church.

(Eph.3:3-6)

3.10 Prophecy will be fulfilled

The things that God says through a prophet will be fulfilled very precisely. If any prophet says that there would be peace and it will be so. When the word of a Prophet comes to pass, then he will be known as the one who is sent by the Lord truly. God didn't allow any of the words of Samuel to fall on the ground and he established him as a Prophet.

Sometimes, even true prophecies may not be fulfilled. The reasons for that are:-

1) If there is **repentance**, the prophecy will not be fulfilled

If people give heed to judgment prophecies and repent, God shows mercy and does not fulfill the prophecy as he did in Nineve.

2) If there is **disobedience** in us, it will not be fulfilled

Moses sang prophetically that all the people of Israel who left Egypt would inherit Canaan. It should be noted that because of their disobedience none of them, except Joshua and Caleb, were able to enter into Canaan.

(Jer.28:9, 18:10, I Sam 3:19,20, Jonah 3:1-10, James 2:13, Ez.33: 14,15, Jer 18:7,8, Ex.15:1,17, Num.14:34, 35)

3.11 Appointment of a Prophet

Prophets are appointed by God at particular times for specific ministries. It was through Moses the Lord brought Israel out of Egypt and he kept them in the wilderness. It was also through Moses that God gave the Law to the Israelites. Furthermore, He gave Moses the task of building the tabernacle in the wilderness showing him the pattern.

For many years, Samuel was involved in judging Israel and was their leader. In addition to this, he also anointed Saul and David as kings. Elijah and Elisha completed the momentous task of eradicating the worship of Baal from Israel. Jeremiah undertook the task of reforming the people for about 23 years before Babylonian captivity. God appointed him to root out, to pull down, to destroy, to throw down, to build, and to plant. He sharply prophesied to them about the Babylonian captivity. In Babylon, when the people of Israel were captives, God appointed Ezekiel to be their **watchman**. It was during the same period God raised Daniel and placed him in a high position to protect his people. God revealed Daniel the end time events. God used a group of prophets – Zachariah, Haggai, and Nehemiah -- to bring back the people of Israel from Babylon to their own country and to rebuild the temple.

John the Baptist prepared the way for the ministry of the Lord Jesus Christ. As the incomparable prophet, Jesus Christ laid the foundation for the doctrines of the New Testament. In the New Testament Church, Apostles and prophets are the foundation stones while Christ is the chief cornerstone. In the early days of the Church, Prophets fulfilled the work of laying the foundation. God used John – an apostle and prophet -- to write, to warn, and to counsel the first century churches which were in a disorderly condition. Two prophets would do the prophetic ministry with signs and wonders for one thousand two hundred and sixty days during the tribulation period. Right now, God continues to appoint prophets, and he is going to do a great reformation work before the perfection of His Church. Even in the present days, God is raising Prophets to root out, pull down, destroy, throw down, to build, and to plant. God is calling prophets who would prophesy to the dry bones. God prepares prophets to see the vision of the pattern of the New Testament Church and to make it known to the churches. God is going to send prophets who would make known the iniquities and transgressions of his people. To put it in a nutshell, the true prophets are shaped by God, are sent by God, and are used by God.

(Hosea 12:13, I Sam.7:13, 10:1, 16:12, 13, I Kings. 19:10,15,17, 21:19-26, 18:21-40, II Kings. 9:1-37, 10:1-28, Jer. 1:10, Ez. 3:17, Dan. 12:4, Luke 3:1-22, Deut 18:18, Rev. 1:19, 2:1-3, 14, 11:1-12)

3.12 The Zeal of the prophets

True prophets are those who stand for God with great zeal. When all people got immersed in Baal worship, Elijah alone, being filled with godly zeal, declared, "This is the true God." He challenged them, "**The god who answers by fire is God.**" Elijah said, "**I have been very zealous for the Lord God of hosts.**"

When the people of Israel made a calf as their god, Moses, with the zeal of God, confronted them saying, "Who is on the Lord's side?" Even though Daniel knew that the Babylonian law forbade him praying to God, it was the zeal of God that caused him to pray thrice a day as per his custom. Even though the prophets may appear to be crazy in the sight of the people, and they are a subject of laughter, mockery, and reproach, but they stand for God. Indeed, they learn to stand alone for God. It is only the zealous men like Elijah can bring God's fire upon the present day churches.

(I Kings. 18:40, 19:14, Ex 32:26, Dan6:10, I Kings. 18:22-39, II Kings 9:11, Jer. 10:7,8, Hosea 9:7)

3.13 Boldness of the prophets

As God is with his prophets as a mighty man of war, they are able to live with a great boldness. Jesus referred Herod as fox and declared that he was ready to die in Jerusalem. Elijah exterminated 450 prophets of Baal who were authorized by the Government. Paul was bold enough to face death. John the Baptist boldly denounced King Herod's sin – perhaps, he was beheaded because of that. Only God's prophets act with unusual boldness in the midst of tribulations. God gives them boldness not to be afraid of any adversity or death. An angel of God emboldened Elijah saying, "The journey is too far for you". God encouraged Jeremiah for a difficult future journey saying, "If you have run with the footmen, and they have wearied you, then how can you contend with horses? And if in the land of peace, in which you trusted, they wearied you, then how will you do in the flooding of Jordan?"

He who is afraid of death or people or powers of darkness cannot undertake the ministry of a prophet. God gives boldness to His prophets and says, "Therefore, prepare yourself and arise, and speak to them all that I command you."

(Jer. 20:5,11, 1:17, Isa. 42:13, Luke 13:32, 33, I kings. 18:40, Acts. 21:13, Mark 6:17, 18, Matt. 14:10, I Kings. 19:7)

3.14 The Prophet's voice of intercession.

The Prophet's prayer differs from the prayers of others. True Prophets are those who have the heart to identify themselves as one among the imperfect people while praying for them. They denounce the faults of people in public, but confess their sins as if they are their own sins when they stand before God in the closet. Thus prayed Isaiah, **"We** are all like an unclean thing, and all **our** righteousness are like filthy rags; **we** all fade as a leaf, and **our** iniquities, like the wind, have taken **us** away… you have consumed us because of **our** iniquities."

Daniel prayed, "**We** have done wickedly and rebelled, even by departing from your precepts and your judgments. Neither have **we** heeded your servants the prophets. **We** have not obeyed the voice of the Lord our God… **we** have sinned, **we** have done wickedly!" He considered the sins of the people as his own. Jeremiah also pleaded, "… For **we** have sinned! … turn **us** back to You, O Lord, and **we** will be restored; renew **our** days as of old".

The prayers that the prophets invoke in God's presence for the people show how tender their hearts are, even though their words seem to be sharp sword. Moses pleaded for the people -- pledging his own life -- saying, "Blot **me** out of your book." The prophet's prayer is for not just bringing earthly blessings from God, it is an interceding prayer for forgiveness of sins, which mends the broken relationship between God and His people.

(Isa. 64: 6, 7, Dan. 9:5-15, Lam. 5:16, 21)

CHAPTER 4

Prophets and Prophesiers

4.1 Prophets

Paul raised a question to Corinthians believers, **"Are all Prophets?"**

We can answer this question in a single word, "No". Paul himself answers this question in the Epistle to the Ephesians that God has appointed only some people to be prophets. Prophetic ministry is for all believers, but the office of a Prophet is only for a few.

(1 Cor. 12:29)

4.2 Prophesiers

The gift of prophecy alone does not qualify anyone to be a Prophet. Most of the believers think that those who have the gift of prophecy are prophets. New Testament prophetic ministry is shared by prophets and prophesying believers. All the prophesying believers are not prophets. Agabus was a prophet while Philip had four virgin daughters who used to prophesy. **They were not prophetesses, but they were**

prophesiers. Paul advised the Corinthian believers to seek the gift of prophecy, but not the office of a prophet. A person cannot become a prophet just because of the experience of prophesying for a long time. Unless he is specifically called to be a prophet, he can't stand in the office of a prophet.

(Eph. 4:11, Joel 2:21, 22, Act. 21:9, 10, 1 Cor. 4:1, 29, Rom. 11:29)

CHAPTER 5

Understanding
The Prophetic Ministry

Although everyone does not have a part in this ministry in the same level, the Church of Christ should be involved in the prophetic ministry. Hence, it is necessary to understand the different levels of prophetic ministry.

5.1 Simple prophecy

First of all, the testimony of Jesus is the spirit of prophecy. Any believer may speak about what the Holy Spirit inspires him for the edification of the church. Even a testimony of Jesus for the edification of others can be called prophecy. This form of prophecy does not need any specific prophetic revelation. But it is released because of the inspiration of the Holy Spirit. All believers may do this kind of prophetic ministry. Apostle Paul says, "For you can **all prophesy** one by one, that all may learn and all may be encouraged."

(Rev. 19:10, 1Cor. 14:31)

5.2 The Gift of prophecy

The second level of prophetic ministry is done by believers who have the gift of prophecy. The gift of prophecy is listed among the nine gifts of the Holy Spirit. In the fourteenth chapter of First Corinthians, Apostle Paul insists thrice the importance of prophesying:

*"I wish... even more that you **prophesied."** (Verse 5)*

*"Desire spiritual gifts, but especially that you may **prophesy."** (Verse 1)*

*"Therefore ... desire earnestly to **prophesy."** (Verse 39)*

All believers are encouraged to seek this gift so that the churches may be built up in the Lord. The gift of prophecy is neither fortune telling (about the future) nor speaking by assumption, but it is speaking the mind of God by the revelation of the Holy Spirit. It is written in the Scripture that Philip had four virgin daughters who prophesied. Manifestation of the gift of prophecy is given to the believers according to the will of the Holy Spirit. This gift may be granted through the laying on of hands by the men of God.

(1Cor. 12:10, 1Cor. 12:7, 11, 2 Tim. 1:6, 1 Tim. 4:14)

5.3 The office of a prophet

We have already seen only a very few have the calling to be a prophet. Prophets play a major role in the prophetic ministry of the New Testament.

- ➢ Prophets are personally called by God.
- ➢ Prophets are given prophetic anointing to prophesy.
- ➢ Prophets are gifts of Christ to the churches.
- ➢ Prophets are appointed by God Himself.
- ➢ Prophets intercede to God for the people of God.
- ➢ Prophets rebuke the people of their sin and lead them to God. Prophets challenge the people to live their lives centered in the Most High God.
- ➢ Prophets warn the people of the imminent danger and calamities. They also make known what shall take place in the future.
- ➢ Prophets use sharp words.

Prophets receive not only the prophetic revelations, but also the prophetic utterances. The very word of God (Rhema) comes directly to them. As it was in the Old Testament days, the prophetic ability to receive the word of prophecy from God and delivering them differs from prophet to prophet. Some of the Old Testament prophets were known as Major Prophets while others were called as Minor Prophets. Those who have a higher degree of prophetic ability, obviously, receive very clear and deeper revelations from God -- about the very important matters under various topics -- can deliver very explicit and authoritative prophecy.

(1Cor. 14:29-32, Jer.1:5, Amos 7:14, 15, Eph. 4:8-11,1Cor. 12:28, 1Sam. 3:19, 20, Num.14:11, 20; 1Sam.12:23; Ps.106:23, 2 Sam. 12:9, Act. 21:11, 11: 27-30, Matt. 24, Isa. 49:2)

5.4 Prophetic Ministry and the Holy Spirit

Apostle Peter said that the holy men of God – prophets – spoke as they were moved by the Holy Spirit. The meaning of the word "moved" is similar to a ship which is moved by the wind. The Holy Spirit is the author of all genuine prophecies. The gift of prophecy is granted to the believers by the Holy Spirit according to His will. Prophecy is one of the results of the outpouring of the Holy Spirit -- both in the Old and New Testament. According to the prophecy of Joel, the youth would prophesy, and this was also quoted by Peter on the day of Pentecost when the Holy Spirit was poured out first on the New Testament Church. The Bible again and again affirms that there is a very close connection between prophecy and the Holy Spirit. On many occasions it was proved in the Scripture that people began to prophesy as the Holy Spirit -- the Spirit of prophecy – fell upon them. We find in the Bible that prophesying is sometimes connected with music too.

(2 Pet. 1:21, Joel 2:28, 29, Acts 2:17, 18, I Cor. 12:9, I Sam. 19:20-24, II Chron. 20:14, Num.11:25, 26, I Kings. 22:24, Hosea 9:7, Micah 3:8, II Kings. 3:15, 16, Luke 1:67, Acts 13:1, 2, II Kings. 3:15)

5.5 Apostles and Prophets

In the New Testament, prophetic ministry is very closely associated with the apostolic ministry. Apostles and prophets are the foundational ministers. Revelations about the Church first came to the Apostles and Prophets. God appointed in the Church first Apostles and then Prophets. Some of the Apostles are also called to be prophets. Paul, Silas and Barnabas are the examples for this. Babylon will mainly be judged because of the apostles and prophets. Jesus Christ specifically prophesied about the persecutions and death that the Apostles and Prophets would suffer.

(Eph. 2:20-22, Eph. 3:5, 1Cor. 12:28, Act. 13:1, 15:32, Rev. 18:20, Matt. 23:34, 24:9)

5.6 Delivery of Prophecies

"The Spirit of the Lord will come upon you and you will prophesy with them and be turned into another man." (I Sam. 10:6)

When the Holy Spirit is poured upon the people of God, they may receive prophetic revelations or prophetic utterances. In the New Testament, when people receive the Holy Spirit, they speak in other tongues and prophesy. Sometimes, a prophetic message may be given through an action, and it is the demonstrative prophecy. Isaiah, Jeremiah, Ezekiel, Hosea and Agabus prophesied in this method. Sometimes the Spirit of God may give a message through prophetic songs. Note the prophetic message in the songs of David and Moses. Knowing the things that are going to happen in the future and praying for them beforehand is the prophetic prayer. The messages given distinctively by the Holy Spirit to write are useful for many years, and they become prophetic writings. Perhaps, Prophets also share prophecies with their emotions.

Some people think that foretelling alone is the prophecy while others insist that forth-telling God's written word alone is the prophecy. In the light of the Bible, we can clearly understand that the New Testament prophetic ministry is a combination of both -- foretelling as well as forth-telling prophecies. Some people teach that the gift of prophecy ceased in the first century because it is written in the Scripture, "We know in part and we prophesy in part. But when that which is perfect has come, then that which is in part will be done away." The 'perfect' mentioned in this verse has not yet come. If it had come, knowledge also would have been done away!" The word "Perfect" denotes the perfection, which is yet to come -- the **full measure** of the stature of Christ. The Holy Spirit will continue to give us the prophetic gifts till the Church reaches this goal.

(Joel 2:28, Acts 13:1-3, 19:6, Jer.27: 13:1, Isa.20:2-4, Ezek. 4:1-3, Hosea 3, Acts 21:10, 11, II Sam. 23:1, 2, Acts 2:29, 30, Exodus. 15:1-18, Jer. 36:4, Rev. 1:18, 19, I Cor. 13:9,10, 13:8-10)

CHAPTER 6

The Difference between the Old and New Testament Prophets

"It is essential to understand the difference between the Old Testament and the New Testament Prophets for a proper recognition of the prophet's function in the New Testament Church."

- Kevin J. Conner

6.1 The Old Testament and the New Testament

In the Old Testament prophets anointed priests, kings and prophets for ministry, whereas in the New Testament God anoints His servants for ministry. The Old Testament Scriptures were written by the prophets while most of the New Testament Scripture portions were written by the Apostles. Old Testament prophets enquired of the Lord and revealed God's will to others because the Holy Spirit had not been granted to live within man. But, in the New Testament, matters already revealed (personally) to believers are affirmed by the prophets.

(Heb. 1:1, II Pet. 1:20, 21)

6.2 New Testament Believers

Some of the New Testament believers are going to the prophets to know about their ministry, calling, marriage and business. This is not the right practice as the Holy Spirit is dwelling in us. He speaks through prophecy to those who are in the five-fold ministry as well as to the believers. But according to God's word, it is to be confirmed by two or three witnesses. For the edifying of the body of Christ, and for the equipping of the saints, we should accept the ministry of the prophets.

The prophetic ministry, which is one among the fivefold ministry, is meant to bring the Church into **perfection**. Doors of the churches must be opened to this ministry as mysteries are revealed specially to the prophets. **The mystery of Christ, which in other ages was hidden to the sons of men, are being revealed now by the Spirit to Apostles and prophets.** Prophets are needed for the Church and for the welfare of the nations. God may even speak to us a new thing through a prophet, which the Holy Spirit did not speak to us earlier. But, we should assure them by praying about it.

(Eph. 4:11-13, 3:4,5, I Cor. 14:3, 13:2, I Pet. 1:10)

CHAPTER 7

Judging the Prophecies

"Do not despise prophecies. Test all things; Hold fast what is good." (I Thes.5:20, 21)

"Let two or three prophets speak, and let others judge." (I Cor. 14:29)

We should not disregard prophecies. At the same time, all believers have the responsibility to test the prophecies. In the first centenary, there were fair-minded believers diligently searched the Scripture (Old Testament books) to find out whether the words preached to them were true. Here are some points to be considered to evaluate the prophecies.

(Acts 17:11)

7.1 Does it agree with the written word of God?

The written word is the touchstone to test all prophecies. The Holy Spirit alone is the Author of the Scriptures. All the prophecies written in the Scripture came from the Holy Spirit – not from the will of men. The Holy Spirit has inspired the holy men of God to deliver those prophecies. Hence, the things that the Holy Spirit reveals now through prophecy will not be contrary to the written word of God. As the Scripture itself is a very sure prophecy, we should ensure that prophecies agree with them. For instance, any prophecy regarding the time and the day of the Lord's coming is contrary to the Scriptures. Be cautious of such prophecies. Jesus said about the day of his coming, "But of that day and hour, no, one knows, not even the angels of heaven, but My Father only". Any prophecy that does not agree with the written word of God doesn't glorify Christ. Concisely, any prophecy that does not glorify Christ Jesus is not from God.

(II Pet. 1:19-21, II Tim. 3:16, 17, Jn.16:13, 14, Mathew 24:36)

7.2 Does the Holy Spirit bear the inner witness within us?

When we listen to the truth the Spirit of God bears witness with our spirit. If any prophecy comes from the Holy Spirit, He Himself will affirm it by His inner witness with our spirit.

"The ANOINTING which you have received from Him abides in you, and you do not need anyone to teach you; but as the same anointing teaches you all things and is true... you will abide in Him."

(Rom. 8:16, I John. 2:27)

7.3 Does it keep us in liberty?

"… Where the Spirit of the Lord is, there is LIBERTY…" (II Cor. 3:17) God never robs the free will of any man. Therefore, any prophecy that steals man's free will and enslaves him does not come from God. **"For you did not receive the spirit of bondage to fear…"** (Rom. 8:15)

7.4 From which spirit does the prophecy come?

True prophecy originates from the Holy Spirit. But prophecies also come from the human spirit and even from the evil spirits. There is an illustration in First Kings Chapter 22. Micaiah prophesied through the Holy Spirit while other prophets prophesied through a lying spirit. Initially, even Micaiah prophesied in agreement with other prophets from his own spirit before delivering God's word. Discerning the spirits that operate behind prophecy is not possible by human ability. The gift of discerning the spirits is the most useful gift to test the spirits behind prophecy because divination is increasing in the name of prophecy in these days. Apostle Paul discerned that the spirits behind the utterance was a spirit of divination.

"Now it happened, as we went to prayer that a certain slave girl possessed with a spirit of divination met us, who brought her masters much profit by fortune telling.

The girl followed Paul and us, and cried out, saying, "These men are the servants of the Most High God, who proclaim to us the way of salvation.

And this she did for many days. But Paul, greatly annoyed, turned and said to the spirit, "I command you in the name of Jesus Christ to come out of her." And he came out that very hour". (Acts 16:16-18)

We should always ensure that by what spirit a person is speaking rather than who is sharing the prophecy. King Saul prophesied by an evil spirit which is recorded in the eighteenth chapter of 1Samuel. But in the very next chapter we see that he prophesied by the Holy Spirit. So the Bible proves that there is a counterfeit prophecy.

(I Kings. 22:15-17, I Sam. 19:23)

7.5 Does it produce Scriptural results?

True prophecy brings edification in the Body of Christ. Any prophecy that brings confusion or controversy is to be evaluated according to the written word of God.

But he who prophesies speaks edification and exhortation and comfort to men. He who speaks in a tongue edifies himself, but he who prophesies edifies the church. (1Cor 14:3, 4)

When they had read it, they rejoiced over its encouragement. Now Judas and Silas, themselves being prophets also, exhorted the brethren with many words. (Acts 15:3, 32)

If the prophecy comes from God, all the believers who listen are inspired, and their hearts are set afire. Prophecy is not given to cause emotional excitement; instead its is meant for our spiritual edification. True prophecy brings conviction of sins to unbelievers – secrets of hearts may be revealed and it may bring repentance. *(I Cor. 14:24, 25)*

7.6 Does it agree with what God has already spoken to us personally?

A prophet who came to Bethel from Judah had personally received orders from God that he should not eat bread or drink water there. But an old prophet came to him saying he too was a prophet and made him eat bread and drink water, and told him that an angel had told him to do so. The innocent young prophet who had failed to check the prophecy of the old prophet lost his life on the way.

Prophet Agabus said, "Thus says the Holy Spirit, so shall the Jews at Jerusalem the man who owns this belt and deliver him into the hands of the Gentiles." This message was similar to the one Paul had already received personally from the Spirit. **Do not accept blindly any prophecy just because it comes from a so called great man of God.** Check them with what God has personally spoken you. Do not accept it if it contradicts with what God has already spoken to you in person.

(1 Kings.13: 8,9,17,24, Acts 20:23, Jer. 23:16)

7.7 Is the prophecy being fulfilled?

"When a prophet speaks in the name of the Lord, if the thing does not happen or come to pass, that is the thing the Lord has not spoken; the prophet has spoken it presumptuously; you shall not be afraid of him." (Deut 18:22)

Whatever God speaks through a prophet will certainly come to pass. God will not fulfill any prophecy that is not from Him. Time will prove that they were spoken from the prophet's own spirit after their own imaginations. In the days of Jeremiah, a man called Hananiah prophesied of his own concerning the Babylonian captivity which was not fulfilled. This method of testing the prophecy is applicable only to the foretelling prophesies. What God speaks through a prophet will have accurate fulfilment. Beware of man-made stuffs being distributed in the name of prophecy.

(Jer. 28:1-17)

7.8 Is the prophecy in agreement with the apostolic doctrines?

"Test all things, Hold fast what is good." (I Thes.5:21)

It is our responsibility to discern whether the prophecy is in agreement with the apostolic teachings. All prophets have to speak without contradicting the apostolic doctrines as they have to acknowledge the writings of Apostles as the commandments of the Lord. Some people like Balaam may share a word of prophecy as the revelation of God. It will also be fulfilled. But, their end will prove who they are. When Balaam's eyes were opened by God, he prophesied excellently about Israel and Jesus Christ. He was indeed the one who heard the voice of God, but his teachings went wrong because of his lust for the money. Balaam's teaching was contrary to God's will. It is true that he was commanded by God not to curse the people of Israel. However, his counsel was contrary to his prophecy. He listened to the teaching of the enemy and counseled king Balak to entice the people of God -- to make them a prey to idolatry and adultery – so that the wrath of God may come upon them to destroy them. Such kinds of teachings were also brought into the New Testament churches even in the first century. Peter also warned the believers to avoid following the ways of Balaam. **Beware of modern prophets like Balaam who twist the apostolic doctrines and turn the Scriptures as they've the art of twisting the word of God.**

God has permitted even Satan to use His word. Satan does not teach the truth hidden in God's word, but teaches his own doctrines to God's people. When he says, "It is written", we should be sound in our minds to say, "It is also written." False prophets also do Bible study and research and entice people with a skillful and scholarly talk in the name of "deeper truths" and spread the false teachings. If we have the sound knowledge of New Testament doctrines we can escape from the deception. Christ Himself **"introduced"** the New Testament doctrines in the four Gospels; Believers **"practiced"** them in the Acts of the Apostles. Apostle Paul

"elaborately explained" them in his Epistles; other apostles (Peter, John, Jude and James) **affirmed** them. The best way to test any doctrines is to study them in the following four angles:-

1) What did Jesus Christ say about this teaching in the **Gospels?**
2) Was this teaching practiced in **the Acts of the Apostles?**
3) How this teaching is expounded in the Epistles of **Apostle Paul?**
4) What do **other Apostles** like Peter, Jude, John and James say about this?

We should rightly discern the word of God. It takes spiritual discernment to identify the deception hidden in the doctrines. Today, we need the study on sound doctrines. A New Testament prophet should not walk alone in his ministry. He should strengthen himself by joining with other prophets and they should minister as a team within the churches as the truth is established by two or three witnesses. Those who do not have the light in them can't speak according to the word.

(1Cor.14: 29, 37, 4:6, John 7:16-18, Math7:21, Isa. 8:20, Num.24:2-4, 17, Jude 11, II Pet. 2:3,15,15, Num.22:20)

7.9 Consequences of wrongly judging the prophecies

We saw earlier how a man of God failed to appraise the words of an old prophet had to lose his life. To assess the prophetic words spiritual maturity and the gift of discernment are highly essential. When people fail to judge the prophetic word rightly they may miss what God has for them, they may go astray from God, they may fail to do God's will, they may get trapped in deception, and they may oppose the negative or unfavourable prophecies.

(I Kings. 13:24)

CHAPTER 8

Identifying False Prophets

The Bible, time and again, warns us about false prophets. There are more warnings given about false prophets than any other false ministry. Jesus said that many false prophets would rise and deceive many. He warned that their signs and wonders would be so deceptive that may even influence the elect ones of God. According to the prophecy of the Lord, rising of many false prophets is one of the signs of the end time; hence, every believer has the responsibility to identify the false prophets. Eventually, a group that prophesies in the name of Jesus Christ will become an outcast to God's kingdom on the Day of Judgment. God permits false prophets in our midst to test us and to know whether we truly love Him and would stand faithful to His word.

(Matt. 24:3, 11, Mark 13:22, Deut 13:3)

8.1 Testing their spirit

"Beloved, do not believe every spirit, but test the spirits, whether they are of God; because many false prophets have gone out into the world." (I John 4:1-6)

One of the methods to detect false prophets is to test their spirits. A true prophet has a genuine born again spirit and he ministers through the Holy Spirit. But the spirits of false prophets are enticing in nature. Jesus said that the false prophets are ravenous wolves inwardly and they would come to God's people in sheep's clothing. Apostle Paul also warned the church at Ephesus that after his departure such kind of wolves would infiltrate the church. It is very important to know the inward characteristic of a false prophet -- he is a devouring wolf inwardly while he puts on the skin of a humble sheep.

(Math 7: 15, Acts 20:29)

8.2 Testing their doctrines

We have already seen in the previous chapter that a true prophet always agrees with apostolic doctrines. John emphasized further that those who are not of God won't listen to apostolic doctrines. False prophets are involved in teaching the false doctrines. Jezebel, a false prophetess taught false doctrines which are contrary to the doctrines of the apostles. Apostolic doctrine says that we should abstain from idols. But, the false prophet who will come in the days of the antichrist, and he would introduce a new idol worship. False teachers and false prophets have been appearing repeatedly in the Church history. Good servants lead people to Christ, but false prophets take them away from Christ. Their sneaky doctrine is contrary to the principles of the Word of God. Be cautious and keep away from such false prophets!

If there arises among you a prophet or a dreamer of dreams, and he gives you a sign or a wonder... comes to pass of which he spoke to you, saying, "Let us go after other gods which you have not known, and let us serve them." You shall not listen to that prophet or dreamer of dreams. (Deut 13:1-3)

(1Thes 5:21, 1Cor 14: 37, 1John 4:6, I John 5:21, Rev. 13:14, 20:20, Acts 15:28, Matt. 7:15, Zech 10:2)

8.3 Testing their spiritual fruits

*"Beware of false prophets, who come to you in sheep's clothing, but inwardly they are ravenous wolves. **You will know them by their fruits**. Do men gather grapes from thorn bushes or figs from thistles? Even so, every good tree bears good fruit, but a bad tree bears bad fruit. A good tree cannot bear bad fruit, nor can a bad tree bear good fruit. Every tree that does not bear good fruit is cut down and thrown into the fire. Therefore **BY THEIR FRUITS, YOU WILL KNOW THEM**"* (Matt. 7:15-20)

False prophets are known by their characteristics which are contrary to the likeness of Christ. Hence, it is our responsibility to discern and identify them. He that has the ways of God, indeed, is a prophet. So we can distinguish between a false prophet and a true prophet by their ways. It is imperative to examine a prophet's personal life. God Himself gave testimony about Moses, the great prophet of the Old Testament: he was more humble than all other men who were on the face of the Earth. Shunammite said about Elisha, "I know that this is a holy man of God". We can identify them not by their gifts, but by their fruits. Consequently, the wolf nature will manifest from those who are in sheep's clothing when God tears away their masks.

(Heb.3:2, Num.12:3, II Kings. 4:9)

8.4 Testing their supernatural manifestations

False prophets, first of all, deceive the people of God with their false appearance. And the next important thing they use is the supernatural power -- although it is similar to the power of God – through which they perform greater miracles, wonders, and signs that may appear to be exorbitant. The appearance of the lawless one will be with the power of darkness, false signs, and deceptive wonders. Those who don't have **the love of the truth** will become prey to the wicked one. Shouldn't we be careful about false signs and wonders? Eventually, in these days, we should sincerely assess whether the signs and wonders are in line with the Word of God. We should solely depend on the Holy Spirit to identify these deceptive wonders and signs of the false prophets.

(II Thess. 2:9, 10, Rev. 13:13,14, Rev. 16:13,14a, Matt. 7:21-23)

8.5 Testing their intentions

*"For I know this that after my departure savage wolves will come in among you not sparing the flock. Also from among yourselves men will rise up, speaking perverse things, **to draw away the disciples after themselves**." (Acts 20:29, 30)*

One of the intentions of the false prophets is to draw the disciples of Jesus Christ towards themselves. True prophets lead people towards God and build the Church of Christ while false prophets have no interest in building up the Church. They are ultimately interested in building up their own kingdoms.

8.6 Beware of them

"Now the Spirit expressly says that in latter times some will depart from the faith, giving heed to deceiving spirits and doctrines of demons." (I Tim. 4:1)

During the tribulation period, a prophet of antichrist will lead people towards universal idol worship. In the last days, many satanic prophets infiltrate the churches to seduce the believers. To protect the local church from the false prophets, at least, a few believers need to have the gift of discerning the spirits. The Elders of the local church have a greater responsibility to safeguard the church from false prophets. Apostle Paul warned the elders at Ephesus that they should take heed to themselves and to their flock. The Elder of the Thyatira church was held responsible for allowing Jezebel to teach and beguile the believers. The warning of Jesus Christ is applicable for all ages of the Church: beware of false prophets. Take heed no one deceives you.

(Acts 20:28-30, Rev. 2:20, Matt.7:15, 24:4)

CHAPTER 9

Female Prophets

9.1 Women Prophets in Old Testament

During the time of the Old Testament, God had placed some women in the prophetic office.

- Miriam, Moses' sister
- Deborah, a judge and mother in Israel
- Huldah
- Isaiah's wife
- Anna, who stayed in the temple

None of the women prophets of Old Testament wrote any portion of the Scripture. In the New Testament no woman prophet name is mentioned as an appointed Prophetess.

"While women might prophesy in a worship service as a charismatic manifestation of the Holy Spirit, which was open to every Christian, no women in the New Testament legitimately held the prophetic office" – Erwin.

(Ex. 15:20, Judges 4:4, II Kings 22:12-20, Isa. 8:3, Luke 2:36-38)

9.2 Women prophets in the New Testament

There is no substantiation in the Bible to prove the ministry of prophetesses in any of the local churches in the New Testament. Anna was an Old Testament prophetess. Jezebel, mentioned in the New Testament was a false prophetess. But women do have a part in the New Testament prophetic ministry. We should clearly understand the difference between prophesying women and woman prophets. The four daughters of Philip were prophesying believers. Paul mentions the prophetic ministry of women in his epistle to the Corinthians. God's promise is, "Your sons and your daughters shall prophesy..."

(I Cor. 11:4, Joel 2:28)

CHAPTER 10

Degraded Prophets

Generally, all the prophets that spoke in the name of God were considered as genuine prophets. But, in the Old Testament there were some degraded prophets. Even in the present day churches such prophets are found. In the Scripture, we find the cry of Prophet Jeremiah, "My heart within me is broken because of the prophets. All my bones shake ... for both prophet and priest are profane; yes, in My house I have found their wickedness, says the Lord. For from the prophets of Jerusalem profaneness has gone out into all the land."

Ezekiel scolded them saying, "O Israel, your prophets are like foxes in the deserts."

(Jer. 23:9,11,15, Ezek. 13:4)

10.1 Commercial Prophets

During the days of Malachi there were prophets who prophesied for money. Balaam loved the wages of unrighteousness. In the end days, false prophets will exploit the believers with enticing words. Judah also prophesied that the false prophets will run greedily in the error of Balaam for profit. Balaam was a gentile and a paradoxical prophet -- whose eyes were opened by God to prophesy about Israel and Jesus Christ -- prophesied for wages and for the sake of money, he went to curse God's children. He commercialized his spiritual gifts. Don't we have such prophets who prophesy prosperity to earn money even today? Spiritual gifts and prayers are sold for money in these days. Prophets like Samuel kept themselves from the love of money. Today, prophesies of health, prosperity, and security are just thrown from the stages with the intention of making money.

(Micah 3:11, II Pet. 2:15, 16, 2:1-3, Jude 11, Num.24:3-17, 1Sam.12: 1-5, Ecc.10:9, I Tim. 6:10, I Cor. 6:9, 10)

10.2 Lying Prophets

Especially, during the days of Jeremiah, there were many false prophets found in Israel about whom Jeremiah spoke explicitly. In those days, there were even women prophets who sew magic charms on their sleeves and made veils for the heads to enslave people. Hannaniah prophesied a lie and caused people to believe it. Those chicanery prophets prophesied lies, false visions, divination, and false dreams to the people of Israel and deceived them. Isaiah called those lying prophets as tail while Ezekiel declared boldly that God was against them. They deceived people by their lying prophecies. It is very important to detect the lie, which comes under the pretext of prophecy.

(Jer. 15:14, 23:14,25, 26, 23:32, 28:1-,11, Isa. 9:15, Ezek. 13:8, 1 Kings. 13:1-24)

10.3 Stealing Prophets

These prophets have not received any word from God personally, but they pretend that as if they have received the Word from God. They actually take the words of other prophets and tell people as their own. During the days of Jeremiah such prophets were rebuked by the Lord, "Therefore, behold, I am against the prophets," says the Lord, "who STEAL My words everyone from his neighbor."

(Jer. 23:30)

10.4 Soothing Prophets

These kinds of prophets do not wish to say hard words to people. So, they cover up the sins of the people by their soothing words and give them false hope. They actually seduce the people of God by saying the words of peace when there's no peace and they try to heal the wounds and hurts temporarily. Even today, such '**band- aid' prophets** are misleading the people and when shall we perceive this truth?

In those days, they strengthened the hands of wicked people and they promised peace and security to them. Don't we have such prophets in our midst these days?

Prophet John the Baptist said sharply, "Even now the axe is laid to the root of the trees. Therefore every tree which does not bear good fruits is cut down and thrown into the fire." Jesus said, "Unless you repent you will all likewise perish." People accept and encourage mostly the comforting prophets. However, God has promised that such prophetic ministry would vanish away. Scrutinize the ministry of true prophets. The Lord sent his prophets to the people of Israel to bring them back to Himself; they severely rebuked the people. Where are the prophets today who can prophesy boldly against the sins and evil ways of the people of God?

(Eze.13:10, Jer.8:11, 23:17, Luke 3:9, 13:5, Ezek.13:10-16, II Chr. 24: 19)

10.5 Visualizing Prophets

Visualization is an art of creating an image or a picture through imagination. Many people make use of this art to get material things or physical needs. These prophets used their visualizing ability to see vain things and prophesied their false visions and vain imaginations to the people as the Word of God. Seeing in the spirit realm through our spirit is different from visualization of the human mind. Many people have failed to differentiate between the two experiences and they're tempted to see their own vain imaginations as visions. In these days, there are many preachers who teach that if you visualize anything again and again in your mind it would come to pass in the real life. This is equal to the occult practice of disingenuous prophets. It's possible for prophets to lead the people of God in a wrong way by false visions.

Prophets should not create visions of their own; they should see visions only from God.

(Jer.14:14, Ezek. 22:28, Ezek. 13:3, Ezek. 13:7, Ezek. 13:16, Isa. 28:7, Lam. 2:14)

CHAPTER 11

Regulation of Prophetic Ministry in churches

11.1 People should prophesy one by one

"Let all things be done decently and in order." (I Cor. 14:40)

When God's Spirit is poured upon the people, they may all prophesy together. But when prophetic ministry is done inside the church, they have to prophesy one by one. "But if anything is revealed to another who sits by, let the first keep silent. For you can all prophesy one by one that all may learn and all may be encouraged?"

(I Cor. 14:30, 31)

11.2 Two or three may speak

"Let two or three prophets speak…" The prophetic ministry should be done in plural. No truth is established by a single person, but by two or three witnesses. To get a complete testimony of a prophetic message, two or three prophets should prophesy, one by one, in churches.

(I Cor.14:29)

11.3 Listeners must weigh the prophecy

"Let others judge." (I Cor. 14:29)
"Do not despise prophecies; Test all things." (I Thess. 5:20, 21)

All believers have to weigh the prophecies according to their spiritual ability of discernment. To weigh a prophecy, one has to listen to it carefully. **'What is being said'** should not be contrary to **'What is written'**. Therefore, the believers who are listening must also be sound in the Scripture.

11.4 Must be said according to the proportion of faith.

"... Whether prophesy; let us prophesy according to the proportion of faith." (Rom. 12:6)

We should know our own measure of faith before we share our prophetic revelations. If we go beyond the measure of our faith, we will get into trouble. Before we prophesy we should have enough measure of faith. When God asked Ezekiel, "Can these bones live?" he said, "O Lord God, You know". It was an answer without faith; however, he prophesied to the dry bones later with faith.

(Ezekiel 37:3, 4)

11.5 Women should cover their head

"Every woman who prays or prophesies with her head uncovered dishonours her head, for that is one and the same as if her head were shaved." (I Cor. 11:5)

This is not just to keep up with the traditions of those days. It is to demonstrate the truth that the Church is submitted to Christ. Moreover, Paul admonished women to cover their head, not for the sake of tradition, but because of the Angels who are watching the manifestations of God's wisdom through the Church.

(I Cor. 11:3, 10, Eph.3:10)

CHAPTER 12

Jesus Christ –
the unique Prophet

➢ Jesus Christ alone is the Most high and unique prophet.

➢ Jesus Christ is the Inter Testament Prophet: John the Baptist was the last of prophets Old Testament. New Testament prophets were granted to the church after the resurrection of Christ. He lived during the time when the two testaments met with each other.

➢ He is the Prophet of prophets.

➢ All prophets prophesied ablout Him. He is the centre of all prophets -- it was only about Him that all prophets testified.

➢ God's word was revealed to the prophets. But, He Himself is the Word of God.

➢ All those who refuse to obey His word will be punished as Moses said that every soul who would not hear that Prophet would be utterly destroyed.

➢ He is the infallible prophet -- although he was in all points tempted as we are he overcame sin. Unlike other prophets, He is the only prophet who knew no sin.

The first prophecy in the Bible is about Him. He came as an incomparable prophet, He went to heaven as the Eternal High Priest, and He will come back as the King of kings.

(Dan. 18:15-22, Heb. 3:2, Act. 10:43, John 1:1-3, Acts 3:23, Heb. 4:15. I Pet. 2:22, II Cor. 5:21, Luke 24:19, Gen. 3:15)

CHAPTER 13

Christ alone is the centre of Prophecies

13.1 Christ and the prophecies written in the Scriptures

Though the prophets have prophesied about individuals, the Church, Nations, Israel and many more things, the 66 books of the Bible make it clear that Jesus Christ alone is the centre of all prophecies. This theme has not been changed both in the Old Testament and the New Testament prophetic ministry.

*And beginning at Moses and all the prophets, He expounded to them in all the scriptures the things **concerning Christ**. (Luke 24:27)*

God has spoken about Christ by the mouth of all His holy prophets since the beginning of the time. The first prophecy that was told in Garden of Eden as well as the last prophetic promise told in the book of Revelation is about the Lord Jesus Christ. His physical birth, His earthly life, His three and half years of ministry, His sufferings, His death, His resurrection, His ascension, being seated at the right hand of God in heaven, sending the Holy Spirit to the Church, living today as the Head of the Church, preparing His bride, His marriage with the New Jerusalem, His second coming, 1000 years reign, judging the earth, and living forever being united with the New Jerusalem are foretold. All the books from Genesis to Revelation have Christ alone as their centre, and this is the special feature of the prophetic ministry.

(Acts 3:21, Gen. 3:15, Rev. 22:20)

13.2 Christ and the present day prophecies

Through prophecy, today, the Holy Spirit gives us words from Christ and glorifies only Him. The Holy Spirit bears the testimony of Christ now. If we look carefully at the present day prophetic ministry, instead of having Christ as the center, importance is given to individuals. Let us go back to the Biblical principles of prophetic ministry. The centre of the prophetic ministry of John was the Lamb of God, and he began to testify about Christ by saying, "Behold! The Lamb of God who takes away the sins of the world." The primary object of a true prophetic ministry is to proclaim Christ, lift Him high, glorify Him alone, and lead people to Him. The testimony of Jesus Christ is also known as the spirit of prophecy.

(John16:11, John 15:26, 1:29, Luke 1:71-80, 2:25-33, 36, 38)

Chapter 14

Prophecies fulfilled
in Jesus Christ

Many prophecies of the Old Testament were explicitly fulfilled in the life of Jesus Christ. It won't be an exaggeration to say that His very life was the life of prophecy. Here, only 42 prophecies I picked up which were fulfilled in His life to prove that Jesus Christ is the true Messiah.

14.1 From the time He was born in Abraham's generation till His ascension to heaven.

1. God the Father foretold that Jesus would be the **seed of Abraham**

"In your SEED all the nations of the earth shall be blessed... (Gen. 22:18)

"The genealogy of Jesus Christ, the Son of David, THE SON OF ABRAHAM" (Math. 1:1)

2. Jacob foretold that he would be born in the **tribe of Judah**.

"... The Scepters shall not depart from JUDAH... until Shiloh comes." (Gen. 49:10)

"It is evident that our Lord arose from JUDAH" (Heb.7:14)

3. Micah foretold that his birth would be in **Bethlehem**.

"But you, BETHLEHEM Ephrathah, though you are little among the thousands of Judah, yet out of you shall come forth to me the One to be ruler in Israel..." (Micah 5:2)

"And Joseph also went up from Galilee, out of the city of Nazareth, into Judea, to the city of David, which is called BETHLEHEM because he was of the house and lineage of David... So it was, that while they were there, the days were completed for her to be delivered. And she brought forth her firstborn Son, and wrapped Him in swaddling clothes, and laid Him in a manger because there was no room for them in the inn." (Luke 2:4, 6, 7)

4. Isaiah foretold that he would be **born of a virgin**.

"Behold the VIRGIN shall conceive and bear a Son, and shall call His name Immanuel (Isa. 7:14)

"The angel Gabriel was sent by God ...to a VIRGIN betrothed to a man whose name was Joseph, of the house of David. The virgin's name was Mary... The angel said to

her, "Do not be afraid, Mary. You shall conceive in your womb and bring forth a Son and shall call His name Jesus." (Luke 1:27-31)

5.   Jeremiah foretold that after His birth **many children would be killed**.

"Thus saith the Lord; "A Voice was Heard in Ramah, lamentation and bitter weeping, Rachel weeping for her children, refusing to be comforted for her children, because they are NO MORE." (Jer. 31:15)
"Then Herod, when he saw that he was deceived by the wise men, was exceedingly angry; and he sent forth and PUT TO DEATH all the male children who were in Bethlehem and in all its districts when from two years old and under, according to the time when had determined from the wise men." (Matt. 2:16)

6.   Hosea foretold that he would go to **Egypt**.

"Out of EGYPT I called My Son." (Hosea 11:1)
"When he arose, he took the young Child and His mother by night and departed for Egypt and was there until the death of Herod." (Matt. 2:14, 15)

7.   Isaiah proclaimed that **the way** would be prepared for Him.

The voice of one crying in the wilderness: "Prepare the way of the Lord. Make straight in the desert a highway for our God. Every valley shall be exalted, and every mountain and hill shall be made low, the crooked places shall be made straight, and the rough places smooth. The glory of the Lord shall be revealed, and all flesh shall see it together, for the mouth of the Lord has spoken." (Isa. 40:3-5)

"As it is written in the book of the words of Isaiah the prophet saying, 'The voice of one crying in the wilderness: Prepare the way of the Lord. Make His paths straight, Every valley shall be filled and every mountain and hill brought low and the crooked places shall be made straight and the rough ways made smooth. And all flesh shall see the salvation of God. And he went into all the region around the Jordan preaching a baptism of repentance for the remission of sins. (Luke 3:3-6, John 1:23)

8. Isaiah foretold that he would be **anointed** by the Spirit of the Lord.

"The Spirit of Lord God is upon Me, because the Lord has anointed Me to preach good tidings to the poor." (Isa. 61:1)

"He saw the Spirit of God descending like a dove and alighting upon Him." (Matt. 3:16)

9. Zechariah proclaimed that he would come **riding on a donkey** in a procession.

"Behold, your King is coming to you; He is just and having salvation, lowly and riding on a donkey, a colt, the foal of a donkey. (Zech. 9:9)

"They brought the donkey and the colt, laid their clothes on them, and set Him on them." (Matt. 21:7)

10. Psalmist foretold that he would have zeal for **His father's house**

"My zeal has consumed me" (Ps. 119:139)
"When He had made a whip of cords, He drove them all out of the temple, with the sheep and the oxen, and poured out the changers' money and overturned the tables. And He said to those who sold doves, "Take these things away! Do not make My Father's house a house of merchandise." (John 2:15, 16)

11. Isaiah foretold that Gentiles would see **His light**.

"Nevertheless the gloom will not be upon her who is distressed, as when at first He lightly esteemed the land of Zebulun and the land of Naphtali, and afterward move heavily oppressed her, by the way of the sea, beyond the Jordan, in Galilee of the Gentiles. The people who walked in darkness have seen a great light; Those who dwelt in the land of the shadow of death, upon them has a light shined" (Isa 9:1,2)

"He came and dwelt in Capernaum, which is by the sea, in the regions of Zebulun and Naphtali, that it might be fulfilled which was spoken by Isaiah the prophet saying ...The people who sat in darkness saw a great light and upon those who sat in the region and shadow of death light has dawned". (Matt. 4:13-16)

12. Psalmist declared that he would speak through **parables**

"I will open my mouth in a parable; I will utter dark sayings of old." (Ps. 78:2)

"All these things Jesus spoke to the multitudes in parables; and without a parable He did not speak to them." *(Matt. 13:34)*

13. Psalmist said that **children** would praise Him

"Out of the mouth of babes and infants You have ordained strength, because of Your enemies, that You may silence the enemy and the avenger." (Ps. 8:2)

"When the chief priests and scribes saw the wonderful things that He did, and the children crying out in the temple and saying, "Hosanna to the Son of David!" they were indignant" (Matt. 21:15)

14. Psalmist declared that He would be a priest according to **the order of Melchizedek**

"The Lord has sworn... You are a priest forever according to the order of Melchizedek." (Ps. 110:4)

"He was called by God as High Priest "according to the order of Melchizedek." (Heb. 5:10)

15. Moses foretold that He would be a **prophet like him.**

"I will raise up for them a prophet like you from among their brethren and will put My words in His mouth, and He shall speak to them all that I command Him." (Deut 18:18)

"...Whom heaven must receive until the times of restoration of all things, which God has spoken by the mouth of all His holy prophets since the world began. For Moses truly said to the fathers, "The Lord you God will raise up for you a Prophet like me from your brethren. Him you shall hear in all things, whatever He says to you." (Acts 3:21, 22)

16. Isaiah prophesied about His three and a half year **ministry**.

"He has sent Me to heal the brokenhearted, to proclaim the acceptable year of the Lord, and the day of vengeance of our God, to comfort all who mourn to console those who mourn in Zion..." (Isa. 61:1-3)

"He began to say to them, "Today this Scripture is fulfilled in your hearing," (Luke 4:18-21)

17. Isaiah foretold that he would be **rejected** by the Jews

"He is despised and rejected by men, a Man of sorrows and acquainted with grief. And we hid, as it were our faces from Him; He was despised and, we did not esteem Him." (Isa. 53:3)

"He came to His own, and His own did not receive Him." (John 1:11)

18. Psalmist foretold that he would **be betrayed** by a close friend.

"Even my own familiar friend in whom I trusted, who ate my bread, has lifted up his heel against me." (Ps. 41:9)

"While He was still speaking, behold, a multitude; and he who was called Judas, one of the twelve, went before them and drew near to Jesus to kiss Him. But Jesus said to him, "Judas, are you betraying the Son of Man with a kiss?" (Luke 22:47, 48)

19. Zechariah foretold that he would be betrayed for **thirty pieces of silver**.

"So they weighed out for my wages thirty pieces of silver. And the Lord said to me, "Throw it to the potter..." that princely price they set on me." (Zech. 11:12, 13)

"He said, "What are you willing to give me if I dewier Him to you?" And they counted out to him thirty pieces of silver" (Matt. 26:15)

20. Psalmist foretold that they would give **false witness** against Him.

"Fierce witnesses rise up. They ask me things that I do not know." (Ps. 35:11)

"They gave false witness against Him." (Mar. 14:58)

21. Isaiah foretold that he would remain **silent** during the time of accusation

"He was oppressed and He was afflicted, yet He opened not His mouth; He was led as a lamb to the slaughter, and as a sheep before its shearers is silent, so He opened not His mouth." (Isa. 53:7)

"And He answered him not one word, so that the governor marveled greatly." (Matt. 27:14)

22. Isaiah foretold that they would **spit on His face and would beat Him**.

"I gave My back to those who struck Me, and My cheeks to those who plucked out the beard; I did not hide My face from shame and spitting." (Isa. 50:6)

"So Pilate took Jesus and scourged Him. (John 19:1)

"Then they spat in His face and beat Him and others struck Him with the palms of their hands." (Matt. 26:67)

23. Psalmist foretold that they would **hate Him without cause.**

"They that hate me without a cause are more than the hairs of mine head: they that would destroy me, being *mine enemies wrongfully, are mighty: then I restored* that *which I took not away." (Ps. 69:4)*

If I had not done among them the works which no one else did, they would have no sin; but now they have seen and also hated both Me and My Father. (John 15:24)

24. Isaiah declared that he would give Himself up as **a trespass offering.**

"He was wounded for our transgressions, He was bruised for our iniquities; the chastisement for our peace was upon Him." (Isa. 53:5)
"who Himself bore our sins in His own body on the tree."(1Pet.2:24)

25. Isaiah proclaimed that he would **carry our sickness**

"Surely He has borne our griefs and carried our sorrows."(Isa.53:4)
"He cast out the spirits with a word, and healed all who were sick, that it might be fulfilled which was spoken by Isaiah the prophet, saying: "He Himself took our infirmities and bore our sicknesses." (Matt. 8:16, 17)

26. Isaiah foretold that he would be **punished along with criminals**.

"He was numbered with the transgressors..." (Isa. 53:12)
"With Him they also crucified two robbers, one on His right and the other on His left." (Mark 15:27)

27. Psalmist foretold that his hands and His feet **would be pierced**.

"They pierced My hands and My feet." (Ps. 22:16)

Then He said to Thomas, "Reach your finger here and look at My hands; and reach your hand here, and put in into My side......"(John 20:27)

28. Psalmist foretold that the **reproaches of others** would come upon Him.

"And the reproaches of those who reproach you have fallen on me." (Ps. 69:9)

For even Christ did not please Himself; but as it is written, "The reproaches of those who reproached You fell on me."(Rom. 15:3)

29. Psalmist predicted that they **would scorn** Him.

"All those who see me laugh me to scorn; they shoot out the lip, they shake the head..." (Ps. 22:7)

"Even the rulers with them sneered, saying, 'He saved others; let Him save Himself if He is the Christ, the chosen of God.' (Luke 23:35)

30. Isaiah foretold that he would **intercede for the transgressors**.

"He poured out His soul unto death, and He was numbered with the transgressors, and He bore the sins of many, and He made intercession for the transgressors." (Isa. 53:12)

Then Jesus said, "Father, forgive them, for they do not know what they do." (Luke 23:34)

31. Psalmist predicted that they would give Him **bitter vinegar** to drink.

"They also gave me gall for my food, and for My thirst they gave me vinegar to drink." (Ps. 69:21)

"They gave Him sour wine mingled with gall to drink. But when He had tasted it, He would not drink." (Matt. 27:34)

32. Psalmist predicted that he would be **forsaken by God the Father**.

"My God, My God, why have You forsaken Me? Why are You so for from helping Me, and from the words of My groaning?" (Ps. 22:1)

And about the ninth hour, Jesus cried out with a loud voice, saying, "Eli, Eli, lama sabachthani?" that is, "My God, My God, why have you forsaken me?" ((Matt. 27:46)

33. Psalmist predicted that **his bones would not be broken.**

"He guards all his bones; not one of them is broken." *(Ps. 34:20)*

"But when they came to Jesus and saw that He was already dead, they did not break His legs." (Jn. 19:33)

34. Zechariah foretold that they **would pierce His side.**

"Then they will look on me who they have pierced." *(Zech. 12:10)*

"... One of the soldiers pierced His side with a spear." *(John 19:34)*

35. Psalmist predicted that they would **cast lots for His clothing.**

"They divide My garments among them, and for My clothing they cast lots." (Ps. 22:18)

"Then they crucified Him and divided His garments casting lots..." (Matt. 27:35)

36. God prophesied that he **would conquer Satan.**

"He shall bruise your head." (Gen. 3:15)

"... through death He might destroy him who had the power of death, that is, the devil." (Heb. 2:14)

37. Isaiah foretold that he would be **buried with the rich**.

"And He made his grave with the wicked and with the rich in His death." (Isa. 53:9)

"Now when evening had come, there came a rich man from Arimathea, named Joseph, who himself had also become a disciple of Jesus. Then Pilate commanded the body to be given to him. And when Joseph had taken the body, he wrapped it in a clean linen cloth, and laid it in his new tomb which he had hewn out of the rock; and he rolled a large stone against the door of the tomb..." (Matt. 27:57-60)

38. Psalmist foretold that his **soul would not be left in Sheol.**

"... you will not leave my soul in Sheol, nor will You allow Your Holy One to see corruption" (Ps. 16:10, 49:15)

"Now this, "He ascended" – what does it mean but that He also first descended into the lower parts of the earth? He who descended is also the one who ascended far above all the heavens, that He might fill all things." (Eph 4:9, 10)

39. Isaiah proclaimed that He would be **raised again from death.**

"He will swallow up death forever." (Isa. 25:8)

He said to them, "Do not be alarmed. You seek Jesus of Nazareth. He is risen! He is not here! See the place where they laid Him." (Mark 16:6, I Cor. 15:4)

40. Psalmist foretold that he would go again to heaven and **sit at the Father's right side**.

The Lord said to my Lord, "Sit at My right hand till I make Your enemies Your footstool." (Ps. 110:1)

"So then, after the Lord had spoken to them, He was received up into heaven, and sat down at the right hand of God." (Mark 16:19)

41. Psalmist predicted that He would give **gifts from above.**

"You have ascended on high, you have led captivity captive; you have received gifts among men, even among the rebellious, that the Lord God might dwell there." (Ps. 68:18)

Therefore, He says: "When He ascended on high, He led captivity captive, and gave gifts to men." (Eph. 4:8)

42. Isaiah proclaimed that Jesus Christ alone would become the **chief cornerstone of the Church.**

"Behold, I lay in Zion a stone for a foundation, a tried stone, a precious cornerstone, a sure foundation; whoever believes will not act hastily." (Isa. 28:16)

"Now, therefore, you are no longer strangers and foreigners, but fellow citizens with the saints and members of the household of God, having been built on the foundation of the apostles and prophets, Jesus Christ Himself being the chief cornerstone." (Eph. 2:19, 20)

CHAPTER 15

World History and fulfillment of Prophecies

The prophecies told in the Bible are precisely and continuously fulfilled in the world history. By this, it is proved that the Bible is an unparallel book of prophecy. Let us see here some of the prophecies fulfilled in history.

15.1 The Fall of Egypt

"It shall be the lowliest of kingdoms; it shall never again exalt itself above the nations, for I will diminish them so that they will not rule over the nations anymore." (Ezek 29:15)

The time the prophecy: 593-571 B.C.

It is true that Egypt, with its long history, was a county with many kinds of special distinguishing merits. It is to be noted that Egypt which was renowned for medicine, science, architecture and natural resources, after the time of Ezekiel lost its competency to rule over other nations. Nebuchadnezzar went to war against Egypt in 472 B.C. and

538 B.C. and plundered it. After that, Egypt never got back its former state. As the River Nile and the Pyramids have become tourist attractions, Egypt has now become a tourist centre. Politically and economically still it lacks behind. Egypt's under development is a proof that the prophecies in the Bible about the Gentile countries are also precisely fulfilled.

15.2. The coming of King Cyrus

"Who says of Cyrus, 'He is My shepherd, and he shall perform all My pleasure, even saying to Jerusalem, "you shall be built" and to the temple, "your foundation shall be laid." (Isa. 44:28)

The time the prophecy: 745-695 B.C.

When Isaiah said this prophecy, the temple was not demolished but was in good condition. After about 100 years, in 586 B.C, Babylon's King Nebuchadnezzar plundered and destroyed the Jerusalem temple. Thereafter, In 539 B.C, the Persian king captured Babylon. Cyrus, king of Persia passed orders that the people of Israel must be set free and that the temple should be rebuilt. The archaeological surveys have affirmed that these incidents had been engraved in the Babylonian stone inscriptions. Truly, we are amazed that Isaiah's prophecy was foretold precisely 150 years before King Cyrus was born, and the temple was not demolished.

(Ezr. 1:1, 2, Isa. 44:28, 45:1-4, 45:13)

15.3 Josiah's ministry of reformation.

"And behold, a man of God went from Judah to Bethel by the word of the Lord, and Jeroboam stood by the altar to burn incense. Then he cried out against the altar by the word of the Lord, and said, 'O altar, altar! Thus says the Lord; 'Behold, a child, Josiah by name, shall be born to the house of David; and on you he shall sacrifice the priests of the high places who burn incense on you, and men's bones shall be burned on you." (I Kings 13:1, 2)

The time the prophecy: 933-911 B.C.

The name of the prophet who said this prophecy is not mentioned. This is a very surprising prophecy, which was foretold about a man, his name, and the ministry he was going to do for the Lord. About 300 years after Jeroboam's days, Josiah was enthroned when he was eight years old. Josiah removed all the abominations that had defiled Israel from the time of Solomon.

"As Josiah turned, he saw the tombs that were there on the mountain. And he sent and took the bones out of the tombs and burned them on the altar and defiled it according to the word of the Lord which the man of God proclaimed, who proclaimed these words." (II Kings 23:16)

This incident is a proof that the history of the world is under the control of the Lord's prophecies.

15.4 The destruction of Tyre

"And they shall destroy the walls of Tyre and break down her towers; I will also scrape her dust from her and make her like the top of a rock. If shall be a place for spreading nets..." (Ezek 26:4,5)

The time the prophecy: 586 B.C.

Tyre was a twin city, in the North West, 60 miles away from Nazareth. One part of it was an island and the other was a fertile land. Nebuchadnezzar waged war against it and brought it under his rule and 13 years later it came under the Persians. Finally, Alexander the great captured it in 532 B.C. It is recorded in history that his soldiers destroyed Tyre and flung everything in it into the Mediterranean Sea. The historian Philip Hyers has written, "Tyre which was once a great city is now just a part of the top of a hill and the greater part of Tyre is just a place where fishermen dry their nets."

Ezekiel's prophecy was that Tyre would be made a desolate city and it was fulfilled surprisingly in the history.

15.5 The destruction of the temple of Jerusalem.

"Then Jesus went out and departed from the temple, and His disciples came to Him to show Him the buildings of the temple. And Jesus said to them, "Do you not see all these things? Assuredly, I say to you, not one stone shall be left here upon another, that shall not be thrown down." (Matt. 24:1, 2)

<u>The time the prophecy: 30 A.D.</u>

In 66 A.D, Jews began to rebel against the Romans. In 70 A.D, under Emperor Titus the Roman army rampaged over them on the day of the Passover. The Emperor Titus not only killed thousands of Jews but also demolished the temple and burnt it. Among the outer walls of the temple only one remains. Jews go to that remaining wall and weep and mourn over it and so it is called the "wailing wall". A mosque has been built in the site of the demolished temple. It is called, "Dome of the Rock."

According to the prophetic words of our Lord Jesus Christ, the Jerusalem temple was demolished within 40 years.

15.6 The Fall of Alexander the Great.

"Then a mighty king shall arise, who shall rule with great dominion, and do according to his will. And when he has arisen, his kingdoms shall be broken up and divided toward the four winds of heaven, but not among his posterity nor according to his domination with which he ruled; for his kingdom shall be uprooted, even for others besides these. (Dan. 11:3, 4)

<u>The time the prophecy: 534 B.C.</u>

Daniel foretold a prophecy many years before, about the kingdoms that would come in the world. There is no doubt that this prophecy was about the king of Greece, the great Alexander. More or less 200 years after this prophecy had been told it was fulfilled in the life of Alexander the Great. After his death (323 B.C.) the Grecian empire was divided into four parts -- Greece, Asia Minor, Syria and Egypt were formed -- and his army captains ruled over those divided kingdoms. How can we deny the truth that the history of the world is shaped by the prophecies of the Lord?

15.7 Sodom's Sin

"Likewise as it was also in the days of Lot" (Luke 17:28)

The time the prophecy: 30 A.D.

The horrible sin that was very much prevalent in the days of Lot was homosexuality. What happened when two angels came one day to Lot's house to dine and stay?

"Now before they lay down, the men of the city, the men of Sodom, both old and young, all the people from every quarter, surrounded the house. And they called to Lot and said to him, where are the men who came to you tonight? Bring them out to us that we may know them carnally." (Gen. 19:4, 5)

Till now, homosexuality has been accepted by the western countries, but recently even India has approved it. Our Lord Jesus Christ foretold in the first century itself that this hideous sin will spread in the end times. It is true that so many have died because of AIDS which was ultimately caused by this evil act and it has been hidden from the eyes of many.

"... For even their women exchanged the natural use for what is against nature. Likewise also the men, leaving the natural use of the woman, burnt in their lust for one another, men with men committing what is shameful, and receiving in themselves the penalty of their error which was due."
(Rom. 1:26, 27)

The prophecy that the Lord Jesus Christ foretold as one of the signs of the end times is being fulfilled speedily in these days.

15.8 Israel's new beginning

"Now learn this parable from the fig tree: When its branch has already become tender and puts forth leaves, you know that summer is near. "So you also, when you see all these things, know that it is near, at the very doors."
(Matt. 24:32, 33)

The time the prophecy was: 30 A.D

For many years, Jews had been troubled by the Gentiles and took refuge in many countries. At one point, Palestine also had become a British colony. At this time, notorious Hitler made a monstrous attack and killed 4 Million Jews. Finally, on May 14, 1948, Palestine got freedom from the British rule. Israel was formed as an independent country. The people of Israel were again gathered together. We know clearly that this incident in the history of Jews is the fulfillment of the prophecy of Jesus Christ. Many of the Jews who were scattered over different parts of the world enthusiastically returned to their motherland to start a new life. The budding of Israel, the fig tree, is a sign that the second coming of Christ is nearer.

15.9 Sixty nine weeks and the slain of the Messiah

"Know therefore and understand, that from the going forth of the command to restore and build Jerusalem until Messiah the Prince, there shall be seven weeks and sixty two weeks: The street shall be built again, and the wall, even in troublesome times. And after the sixty two weeks Messiah shall be cut off..." (Daniel 9:25, 26)

The time the prophecy: 550 B.C

The angel told Prophet Daniel the secret of the 70 weeks. God had already decided that the time between the Babylonian captivity of the people of Israel and the coming of the Messiah would be more or less 69 weeks (7+62=69). After about 70 years of slavery, the people of Israel returned in three groups, that is in the years 536 B.C. (Ezra 1:1-4), 457 B.C. (Ezra 7:11-16) and 444 B.C. (Nehemiah 2:1-8) from Babylon. The prophecy was that after returning of the people of Israel to their own country from Babylon, it would take seven weeks plus sixty two weeks, around 69 weeks, for the killing of Messiah. Biblical scholars reckon that one week denotes 7 years, 69x7= 483 years. This period came to an end around 30 A.D. the year in which the Messiah died on the cross. These prophecies were so precisely fulfilled in the History to prove that the Holy Bible is an incomparable book.

CHAPTER 16

The Unique Life of a Prophet

16.1 They reflect the characteristics of God

Prophets are those who reflect God's characteristics in their own lives to their generation.

Both in the Old and the New Testament, it is only the prophetic ministry that has gone through more persecution than other ministries. The life of the prophets is very specific, different and tough. In the Old Testament days, those who were anointed as kings lived luxuriously in the palaces while Priests served in the temple with the financial support of other eleven tribes. But, prophets were like vagabonds, tormented by kings, abandoned by the people, and were on the run. Neither any palace nor the Temple accommodated them. In their own house as well as in their own native town, they had no respect.

They have to go where God sends them and say only what God asks them to say. If they go out, after getting a negative signal from God, a donkey may advise them. If they do not go where God asked them to go, but try to go somewhere else, they may have to travel in the belly of a fish. Even in their eating, there was God's control. God instructed Ezekiel regarding the quantity of water he should drink and how he should bake the cake. His sleeping posture was also restricted. There was a restraint to express his feelings, even when his beloved wife died. For an allotted time he had to be dumb. Hosea got an appalling order in the matter of his marriage. The order that came to Isaiah was to remove the cloth from his body and to take the sandals off his feet. John had to separate himself from society and live alone in the desert for many years.

If they give the words of God people would snarl; if they don't speak the blood of the people would be upon them; if he keeps it to himself God's word would burn in his bones. If he wants to leave the world, God's voice would say, 'your journey is too far to go.' Even the raven will serve food in the days of famine -- Elijah had to eat that food to survive. In the New Testament also, prophets are called to live a separate life given by God. The life of a Prophet is several times tougher than his ministry. God's revelations and visions penetrate into his life and cause deeper impacts. God matures his life by rejecting his likes, his thoughts, and his own goals. God Himself prepares his circumstances and rules over his life. It is true that God Himself designs the life of a prophet in accordance with His will. If we keenly observe a prophet's life we can find that God takes all decisions for him. Jeremiah confessed that the way of a man is not in himself, and the steps of a man are directed by God.

When we look at the lives of the prophets we can understand that they live under God's resolutions -- God decides to whom they should go and who should come to them. He sent Moses to Egypt, and He also sent Aaron from Egypt to meet him on the way. Though there were many widows -- when there was a famine -- Elijah was sent to a widow who lived in Sarepta. Similarly, Naaman, a Syrian leper, was sent to Elisha to get healed while there were many lepers living in Israel. The message of the prophets comes not only out of his mouth but also out of his life. The message of God flows through the very life of the prophets.

"Every bit of the truth that they give out in word is something that has had a history. They went down into the depths and they were saved by that truth. It was their life, and therefore it is a part of them. That is the nature of prophetic ministry."

T. Austin Sparks

As the Israelites rejected the prophets the present day churches also discard them. People are satisfied with the ministry of pastors in the church and with the ministry of evangelists outside the church. Due to fear they even teach that prophetic ministry ceased in the first century itself. In the New Testament, many broadminded people have made the prophet's place common by saying that all those who prophesy are prophets. Irrespective of the hard life that the prophets go through God performs exceptional things for them. For the sake of a single prophet God would even divide Jordon into two.

(Ezek.4:9-11, Ezek4:4-8, Ezek 24:15-27, Ezek.24:25-27, Hos.1:2, 3, Isa. 20:2, Jer. 10:23, Luke 4:25-27, I Cor. 12:29)

CHAPTER 17

Prophetic Ministry and Spiritual Warfare

17.1 God-appointed Warfare

The first prophecy came straight from God's own mouth, in the hearing of Adam and Eve in the Garden of Eden. God prophesied to Satan, and thus he began the prophetic ministry by saying, "And I will put enmity between you and the woman, between your seed and her Seed; He shall bruise your head, and you shall bruise His heel." (Gen. 3:15)

The important message of the first prophecy was about spiritual warfare. God Himself created enmity between Satan and Israel – the word woman signifies the people of Israel. So, in the history, the people of Israel were attacked many times. The enemy used people like Pharaoh and Haman to exterminate them totally. But, God defeated all his efforts. He also created enmity between Jesus Christ, the seed of Israel and Antichrist, the seed of Satan. It is clear that God declared the spiritual war in the first prophecy. God nullified all the efforts the enemy that he took to prevent the birth of Christ. The prophecies clearly stated that Jesus Christ would be born in the tribe of Judah – specifically, in David's posterity. Through Queen Athaliah, of the royal family of Judah, the enemy tried to kill all the royal heirs of Judah, but God's hand rescued Joash. He unequivocally challenges His enemy and fulfills His plans. When Jesus, as the Lamb of God, laid himself on Calvary's Cross, He simultaneously conquered "the author of death" by His own death. When He was crucified on the cross, He bruised the enemy's head and disarmed the principalities and powers -- having made them a public spectacle -- and triumphed over them.

He also snatched the keys of Hades and death from the enemy. Though Christ defeated the enemy on the cross, the war still continues between the two kingdoms. Bruising of the feet of Christ symbolically represents the war between the enemy and the Body of Christ and Apostle Paul confirms it by saying that we wrestle against principalities, against powers, against the rulers of the darkness of this age, against spiritual hosts of wickedness in the heavenly places. The spiritual warfare is constantly going on between the Church and the powers of darkness. According to God's word, He would crush the enemy under the feet of the Church shortly. The corporate man child will overcome him by the blood of the Lamb and by the word of his testimony. The victory of Christ is the ultimate victory of the Church. God the Father continues to give us the victory through the Lord Jesus Christ, leading us always in triumph in Jesus, and he keeps us through Christ as more than conquerors. The Spirit of the Lord lifts up a banner against the enemy and the gates of Hades shall not prevail against the Church which is being built by Christ.

Prophecies make it clear that the final stage of the war between the Church and Satan would become much intensive. God is going to raise up a group of overcomers out of the end time Church -- she would ultimately give birth to a male child while Satan would be waiting before the woman to devour her child. Who is this male Child? It's not a physical child, but it signifies the spiritual corporate man -- composed of the triumphant believers who would receive God's authority to rule all nations with the rod of iron. Remember that one of the promises of God for over comers is the power and the enthronement to rule over the nations.

Ascending to the throne of God will take place as soon as the manifestation of the male child.

Soon after this event, a war will break out in heaven between Satan and Michael and Satan and his angels would be dislodged from their positions. At that time, a loud voice in heaven would declare the victory of the saints: **they overcame him by the blood of the Lamb, and by the word of their testimony, and they did not love their lives to the death**. Knowing that the accuser has very little time left, he would be furious and would persecute the woman who gave birth to the male child. Afterwards, he would give his power, his throne and great authority to the beast and it would make war with the saints. Anti- Christ would jointly rule with Babylon and the ten kings. After two prophets finish prophesying for thousand two hundred and sixty days (31/2 years), he would make war with them, overcome them and kill them. At the end of his rule, Lord Jesus Christ Himself will come, will make war with him, and will overcome him and his armies -- as the Lord of Lords and the king of kings. He will legally arrest the beast and the false prophet and cast them alive into the Lake of fire. Jesus will put Satan into a prison called bottomless pit. After one thousand years of imprisonment, Satan would be released from the prison for a while. Finally, he and his angels would be cast into the lake of fire and brimstone which is the second death.

In many Scriptures, Prophets spoke about the spiritual warfare. Can anyone deny the fact that the prophetic ministry is linked with spiritual warfare? When the Kings of Israel went to the battlefield, prophets encouraged them and counseled them about war strategies. Prophetess Deborah emboldened Barak, Elisha informed Ahab beforehand about the attack of the Syrian army, and delivered the Israelite army. Jeremiah counseled King Jehoiakim when the armies of the Babylon came against Israel.

God surely encourages us in today's spiritual warfare through the prophecies. Even strategies of war may be made known to us through prophecy. We can even be warned by specific prophecies about the traps and attacks of the enemy. The church in Smyrna was told by prophecy that some of them would be thrown into prison, and they would have tribulation for ten days. When some disciples told Paul through the Spirit (in the city of Tyre) not to go up to Jerusalem and Paul stayed there for seven more days. Paul prophetically informed the Ephesians elders that among them some men would rise up, speaking perverse things and draw away the disciples after themselves. Today also we need the prophetic ministry to stand in the spiritual warfare and to involve in the war with the assurance of victory. Christ has already earned the victory for the church and now it's our responsibility to inherit his victory. He has already prepared for us the table of victory before the enemies.

(II Chron. 22:9-12, Col. 2:15, Eph. 6:11-13, Rom. 16:20, II Cor. 1:14, Isa. 59:19, Matt. 16:18, Rev. 13:6-8, 19:11, 19-21, 12:4-11, 2:26,27, 3:21, 13:1-18, 11:7, 17:1, 2,8-11, 2:10, Acts. 21:4)

CHAPTER 18

Prophets in the Battlefield

18.1 War with Baal and false prophetess

The Bible shows a clear picture of how the prophets were directly involved in the spiritual warfare in the days of the Old Testament. During the days of King Ahab, who reigned over Israel for twenty years, the clouds of spiritual war surrounded Israel, and raised up Prophet Elijah. Ahab not only did evil in the sight of the Lord more than all who were before him but also was involved in more sins than the sins of Jeroboam. He married a daughter of Ethbaal (Ethbaal means the one who lives with Baal) the king of Sidon. He dared to marry a gentile girl who worshipped Baal. Unequivocally, his marriage with a Baal worshipper was a big downfall in his life, and he sold himself to do wickedness in the sight of the Lord as his wife stirred him up. Ahab's palace became the fortress of the spirits of darkness -- fornications, idol worship, sorcery, false accusations and murders originated from there.

Ahab was the doorway for Baal worship which spread speedily into Israel and Judah. He functioned as a hireling of the spirits of darkness. 450 prophets of Baal and 400 prophets of Asherah were fed at Jezebel's table. Ahab supported the false Prophetess in leading the whole Israel into Baal worship along with 850 prophets. Notorious Ahab not only introduced Baal worship to Israel but also to Judah. He made friendship with the Jewish King Jehosaphat who feared God and got her daughter married to his son Jehoram. Through this marriage, the Baal worship penetrated into Judah also. When the darkness overshadowed Israel and Judah, God raised a zealous prophet Elijah -- a man of fire. He was not only a prophet but also a horseman who waged the spiritual war. Along with Elijah, God also used Elisha, Jehu, Michaiah, Hazael, and Jehoiada in the war against the powers of darkness.

This spiritual warfare continued step by step for several years. The first stage of God's war was to nullify the benefits of Baal worship. Baal means "god of prosperity". God wanted to teach a lesson to Ahab that there won't be any material prosperity because of Baal worship. In those days, Elijah prophesied to Ahab that there won't be rain. He also prayed earnestly that God should stop the rain, and there was no rain for three and half years. God ultimately turned down the economy of the country, and the famine was severe in Samaria. As the people suffered for about three years of famine, God said to Elijah, "Go, present yourself to Ahab, and I will send rain on the earth." Before sending rain on the parched land, God wanted his people to turn back to Him, and this is the second stage of the war.

Elijah met Ahab and told him to gather the four hundred and fifty prophets of Baal and the four hundred prophets of Asherah. **"The God, who answers by fire, is God"**, was the challenge. He placed this challenge before them according to God's choice and word. The prophets of Baal accepted this challenge and made sincere efforts to prove that Baal is God -- false prophets also can bring down the fire from the sky and do great miracles before men. On that day, God prevented Baal's fire coming down and he put the powers of darkness to shame. When Elijah called unto God, He sent the fire and proved that He is, indeed, the true God. Consequently, the 450 prophets of Baal were executed on the shores of the brook Kidron. Literally, Elijah acted as a horseman. After the prayer of Elijah it rained; people repented and confessed that Jehovah is God. But, King Ahab and his wife did not turn to the Lord. Instead of repentance, she decided to take away Elijah's head. On hearing the threatening words of the queen, he fled to Horeb, where God revealed him the next stage of war plans – to anoint Jehu as the king over Israel and Elisha as a prophet in his place.

(I Kings16:29, 21:25, 21:26,19:14,17:18, II Chr. 19:2, 17:3-6, 18:1, 20:20, 26-32, 22:10, 22:8-12, 21:6,13, 22:3-5, Micah17, 18, II Kings 8:26, 27,11:1-3, 2:11, I Kings. 16:32, 33, 17:1, Jam.5:17,18, II Kings 2:12, I Kings 18:5, 6,18:1, 17:9-16, 18:22-24, 18:36,18:38,18:40,18:41-46, 19:15, 6, 19:1-8, Rev. 13:13)

18.2 God's Strategies of war

Elijah fought the war alone for some time. After bringing down the fire, God shared a few more vital secrets and strategies of war with Elijah. Today also God similarly reveals his strategies to His prophets. God connected three more persons with Elijah to resist and fight the powers of darkness. Spiritual warfare is not individual, but it's a corporate war. When men of God corporately involve in the war, their strength is multiplied. These four men were the instruments used by God in the war that God himself was waging against Ahab. Straight away from the Mount Carmel, Elijah went to Elisha and appointed him as a prophet. Elisha prophesied to Hazael as a king of Syria, and also became the king later.

Jehu means Jehovah is He. After Ahab's death, Ahaziah ruled for two years and died. Then Jehoram (another son of Ahab) came to the throne and ruled for twelve years. Hence, it took more than fourteen years to anoint Jehu as the King over Israel. Practically, neither Elijah nor Elisha could anoint Jehu. Finally, Elisha sent one of the sons of the prophets to anoint Jehu, who overthrew the powers of darkness.

(I Kings. 19:17, II Kings. 8:13, 9:1-10)

18.3 Ahab's reluctance

Though God had planned to set the people of Israel free from the bondage of darkness, He had patiently waited till the matter of Naboth's vineyard came to the scene. The king became upset when Naboth refused to give him the vineyard. The ambitious and aggressive queen who came to know about this matter promised him that she would make it possible -- she quickly devised a plot without the knowledge of the king and cunningly killed Naboth and his sons. Elijah charged him saying, "You have sold yourself". He was held responsible for all the sins committed in the palace. He built up the Jericho city which God had utterly destroyed. Following the idol worship, sorceries, fornications, false accusations, blood thirst, and abuse of authority were all in full swing at the palace. Ahab disregarded God-given headship, sold himself to the false authority, and finally destroyed himself.

(I Kings.21: 1-16, 2:25,21:18,19, 21:20, Rev.2:20)

18.4 Starting Judgments

Firstly, God's judgment came upon King Ahab at the appointed time. Ahab had gone to fight the Syrian army changing his identity and entered the battlefield. When a man threw an arrow at random, and unknowingly it struck the king of Israel and that brought an end to his life. Leadership is inseparably blended with responsibility and accountability. He viewed and treated God's prophets as enemies.

Secondly, judgment came upon Ahaziah, one of the sons of Ahab. He ruled only for two years. Even when he fell sick, he continued to seek Baal. But, Elijah prophesied voluntarily saying, "Is it because there is no God in Israel that you are going to inquire of Baal- Zebub, the god of Ekron? Now therefore thus says the LORD: "You shall not come down the bed to which you have gone up, but you shall surely die." Ahaziah sent 50 men twice to capture Elijah, and they were all consumed by the fire. Then for the third time, he sent to him a captain of fifty with his fifty men, God asked Elijah to go with them. He went to the palace and delivered the same prophecy to Ahaziah who was on his bed. Though Elijah's head was already targeted they couldn't do anything – he had the strong protection of the mighty hand of God. According to the word of the Lord delivered by Elijah, the unrepentant Ahaziah died.

Thirdly, God's judgment fell upon Ahab's son-in-law, Jehoram who walked in the way of Ahab, his father-in-law. Elijah wrote a letter of prophecy to Jehoram stating that God would execute judgment upon him, his wife and children. Perhaps, he also died in accordance with the prophecy of Elijah and his son Ahaziah became the king of Judah.

Fourthly, God's judgment came upon Joram (also called Jehoram), another son of Ahab, and upon Ahaziah, son of Athaliah. Joram ruled over Israel. Although the Lord's prophets helped him several times, he avoided them. He only sought the prophets of other foreign gods. When he came to Elisha, he became upset and said, "What have I done with you? Go to the prophets of your father and the prophets of your mother." As Joram also did not repent in the twelve long years granted to him God's wrath came upon him. No sooner the Lord anointed Jehu he went straight from the war front to meet Joram who got wounded in the war and was resting in Jerusalem. At this time, Ahaziah, the king of Judah came to visit him. Ahaziah did not come there accidentally, but according to the sovereignty of God. Jehoram happened to meet with Jehu on Naboth's land. And Jehu finished him there. Seeing this, Ahaziah tried to run away. But, Jehu chased him and finished him too.

Following this, judgment came upon Ahab's wife. Many opportunities were given to the princess of Sidon who never knew God. Having been caught in the web of the powers of darkness she spread the worship of Baal speedily in Israel, killed the Lord's prophets, and increased fornication and sorcery. As soon as Jehu entered the palace he commanded the guards to throw her down. According to the word of Elijah, her story precisely ended on that day. Obviously, God is a consuming fire and it's a fearful thing to fall into the hands of the living God. Jehu carried out a mission of judgment that was in God's heart-- he completely destroyed the strongholds of the powers of darkness. God continues to wage spiritual warfare in the days of the New Testament also by raising people like Jehu to pull down strongholds, to cast down arguments against the knowledge of God, and to bring every thought into captivity to the obedience of Christ.

(II Kings. 1:3, 4, 6, I Kings 22:34,1:2-16, II Chron. 20:32, 21:12-15, I Kings. 21:12, 13, II Kings. 3:13, 9:17-25, 9:27, 9:7, 22, 30-33, 9:30-37, 10:11, Heb. 12:29, I Pet. 4:17, Rev. 2:20-23, II Cor. 10:3-5)

18.5 Abolition of Baal worship

Jehu removed Baal worship completely -- He went to all the places, wherever the temples of Baal existed, brought the idols and sacred pillars out of the temples of Baal and burned them – and his captains broke down the sacred pillars of Baal and tore down the temples of Baal, and made it a refuse dump. All the prophets, servants and priests of Baal were destroyed. God has wiped off the family of Ahab to uproot the Baal worship from Israel. To liberate Israel from Baal, God waged a war for longer time and gave His people a complete victory.

Finally, God's judgment came upon Ahab's daughter Athaliah. When Athaliah knew that her son Ahaziah had been killed by Jehu, she arose and destroyed all the royal heirs as revenge. Only a little boy Joash escaped as Jehoiada, the priest hid him. She captured the throne and ruled for six years. Jehoida killed her when the right opportunity came. Why did Athaliah want to destroy the royal heirs of Judah? The enemy knew that Jesus Christ would be born in the tribe of Judah; hence, he plotted to kill the royal heirs through Athaliah. After her demise, Baal worship was totally removed from Judah.

"Three battlegrounds," a book written by Francis Frangipane is very useful to clearly understand and know about the spiritual warfare of the present day Church. Other two books, written by Dr. Rebecca Brown, "He came to set the captives free" and "Prepare for war" give a clear picture of the present day spiritual warfare. The very same spirits of darkness that operated against Israel in the days of Ahab are working against the Church right now. In the intensive war of the last days, warriors like Elijah and Elisha will rise to inherit the victory. In this battle, each believer generally fights to safeguard themselves – as a defensive warfare -- while prophets enter into the enemy's fortress and make counter-attack – as an offensive warfare -- to completely dislodge them.

(II Kings. 10:26-28, II Kings. 10:18-25, Eph. 6:12)

Chapter 19

Elijah Again

19.1 The Excellence of Elijah

And Elijah the Tishbite, of the inhabitants of Gilead, said to Ahab, "As the Lord God of Israel lives, before whom I stand, there shall not be dew or rain these years, except at my word". This was the introduction of Elijah.

He introduced himself to Ahab as the one who stands before the Lord God of Israel. Elijah identified himself with God. First of all, he stood before God. He lived with the God who is a consuming fire, and he also become a fire. He proved that Jehovah alone is God by bringing fire down. He brought fire down and destroyed Ahab's army and its captains. There were chariots of fire and the horses of fire separated Elisha from Elijah. His tribe was not mentioned anywhere, and we don't know anything about his family background. He was known as a Tishbite of Gilead. It seems that he was just an ordinary man. He suddenly appeared before the king one day and delivered a negative prophecy boldly that there would not be any rain and disappeared for three and a half years. Elijah stood not in the strength of his family background, but in God's strength.

Look at Elijah's appearance: He was a hairy man and wore a leather belt around his waist. This is also a sign that he did not concur with the world. John the Baptist, who should have worn a priest's garment and served in the temple, also appeared just like Elijah. John who had Elijah's spirit and strength wore camel's hair with a leather belt around his waist. Elijah and John changed not their appearance for the sake of the people --they did not like to be the modern day prophets with ostentatious appearance, degrees and commendations and learnt their theology in the desert.

John was rigid in his speech while preparing the way for the Lord. He addressed the people as the brood of vipers, cautioned them that the axe was laid at the root of the trees, and proclaimed the judgment of God saying that God would burn up the chaff with unquenchable fire. He convicted the people using harsh, thunderous words such as, "Every tree that does not bear good fruit is cut down and thrown into the fire, the chaff He will burn with unquenchable fire." People won't come to the meetings of preachers who speak in such tones! But, the truth is that through this kind of preaching, people turned to God, confessed their sins, and were baptized. Jesus testified about John, "among those born of women there has not risen one greater than John the Baptist." Elijah stood against Baal and proved that the Jehovah is God. People repented. The need of this hour is the sermons of repentance and remission of sins that convict the people about sin, righteousness and judgment.

Elijah scolded Ahab, "**You have troubled Israel. You have sold yourself.**" John the Baptist also, with the same defiance, rebuked Herod for the illegitimate relationship he had with his Brother Philip's wife. Whereas, in these days Christianity is accepting pre-marital sex, extra- marital sex, divorce, illegitimate remarriages, marriages of homosexuals and lesbians. We need men like Elijah who would raise their voices against such sins. The Spirit of Elijah will not compromise with idolatry, fornication, witchcraft. John the Baptist, did not care even for his life, but pointed out the sin and rebuked it. These kinds of men align themselves perfectly with the Holy Spirit, who convicts the world of sin, righteousness, judgment, and act accordingly. There's a great need today for men of God like Elijah who would stand for God with a strong heart and backbone! Elijah's spirit lifts up Christ and glorifies Him with the cry, "He must increase and I must decrease". We need men like Elijah to prepare the Church for the second coming of the Lord.

Prophets are not those who please people living in sin and comfort them. There was silence in Israel for 400 years. There was no prophet to declare God's word saying, "Thus say the Lord of Hosts." The coming of John the Baptist once again brought God's fresh word to Israel. When Annas and Caiaphas were high priests, the word of God came to John in the wilderness. **Prophets like Elijah and John wait till the Word of the Lord comes to them in Person.** John the

Baptist came with the spirit of Elijah, but the people thought that he was demon possessed.

(I Kings. 17:1, II Kings. 1:8, Matt. 3:4, 11:14, 17:11-13, Lu.1:15-17, 3:9,2-6,16,17, Matt.3:2-12,7,11:11, I Kings. 18:37-39, Luke 24:47, 3:19, Rom. 1:26, 27; I Cor. 6:9; Gal. 5:19; Lev. 18:6-23; 20:10-21; Deut 27:20-23, John 5:35, Matt. 11:18)

19.2 Will God send Elijah again?

We see that during the reign of the Antichrist two prophets will minister with the power of Elijah. They will be able to change water into blood and afflict the world will all plagues as in the days of Moses. At the same time, as it happened in Elijah's days, they will be able to destroy the enemies with fire and shut up the sky from rain. Before the second coming of Christ, there should be a work of preparation. It is clear that Elijah group of prophets are again needed for that ministry.

"Behold, I send My messenger, and he will prepare the way before me... But who can endure the day of His coming?"

"Behold, I will send you Elijah the prophet, before the coming of the great and dreadful day of the Lord. He will set things right."

In the last days, God will raise the group of Elijah like prophets with the prophetic anointing to herald the message of repentance, to move against the fortresses of darkness, and to break up the fallow ground before the end-time revival. We can observe that the prophetic letter of John – The book of Revelation -- contains the message in the style of Elijah.

(Rev. 11:5-7, Mal. 3:1, 2, 4:5, 6, Hosea 10:12)

CHAPTER 20

The Afflictions of Prophets

"Take the prophets, who spoke in the name of the Lord, as an example of suffering and patience." (James 5:10)

When a prophet speaks exactly what God wants him to speak it makes some hearers uncomfortable. People are pleased with the prophets who speak what is comfortable to them. It is evident that in the day to day life people dislike prophets who speak what is pleasing to God. Prophets are also subjected to tribulation just because they do what God tells them to do. During the journey of wilderness, at one point, Moses felt his condition was utterly miserable that he cried to God, "The burden is too heavy for me. If you treat me like this, please kill me here and now. If I found favor in your sight and do not let me see my wretchedness." Elijah also went through the similar experience when he went a day's journey into the wilderness and sat under a broom tree. And he prayed," It is enough! Now, Lord, take my life". Another incidence found in the life of Jeremiah confirms the afflictions of the prophets, "Cursed be the day in which I was born! ...Why did I come forth from the womb to see labor and sorrow, that my days should be consumed with shame?"

(Num.11:11-15, I Kings 19:4, Jer. 20:14-18)

20.1 Oppositions

Who stand against the prophets? Those who oppose God ultimately oppose his prophets. The perverse hearted Israel, being disobedient to God, opposed Moses many times in the desert. On hearing the prophecy, some people get excited while others hate. Sometimes they repent; sometimes' they get furious and oppose. The king, priests and the people opposed Jeremiah when he foretold the Babylonian captivity, and they decided to kill him. Amaziah stood against Amos and obstructed him from prophesying. It is certain that even in these days, many people will oppose true prophets who stand for God and tell His Words. All those who build Babylon inside the Church will oppose the true prophets. It is an undeniable truth that when God meets with them those who oppose pay a heavy price.

20.2 Dishonor

All people do not accept prophets as they accept other servants of God. Generally, people treat prophets not with due respect. We find that Jesus Christ Himself went through the rejection and dishonor as a prophet. The crowd saw Christ as a carpenter and a carpenter's son; they dishonoured him, and labeled him as mad and demon possessed. But, God supplies strength to His prophets to endure the sufferings brought by dishonor. The calling, gifts, and teachings of the prophets are subjected to many kinds of questions. It is not necessary for a true prophet to prove that he is a prophet called by God to those who dishonour him -- proving the calling is God's work.

(Matt.13:55-57, Mark 6:5)

20:3 Intimidations

King Amaziah brought the gods of Seir and set them up to be his gods and bowed down before them. Therefore, the anger of the Lord was aroused against Amaziah, and He sent a prophet to him who said to him, "why have you sought the gods of the people which could not rescue their own people from your hand?" The king threatened him saying, "Have we made you the king's counsel? Cease! Why should you be killed?" We know how Elijah was threatened after the repentance of the people.

(II Chr. 25:16, I Kings 19:20)

20.4 Imprisonment

When sins are openly exposed, a warning is given, and repentance is preached, a few people receive a spiritual revival while others are vexed and they try to punish the prophets. This has been happening since the beginning of time when the prophetic ministry was known. As Micaiah conveyed the words of God, Zedekiah struck him on the cheek. Ahab ordered to push him in prison and to feed him with the bread of affliction and water of affliction.

Hanani, a seer, came to Asa King of Judah, and told a prophecy which provoked the king, and he declared imprisonment for him. When Pashhur, the priest, heard about the prophecy of Jeremiah, he struck him and put him in stocks in the house of the Lord. King Zedekiah again put Jeremiah in prison. Later on, they took Jeremiah and cast him into the dungeon where there was no water but mire. We know well that John the Baptist was imprisoned because he pointed out the sin of Herod. Jesus Christ has warned that this would happen time and again. "I send you, prophets, wise men, and scribes; some of them you will kill and crucify, and some you will scourge in your synagogues and persecute from city to city."

Sometimes, Prophets are being kept as prisoners by the circumstances with all their authorities and rights seized and being tortured is also similar to the physical imprisonment. Prophet John being in the isle of Patmos was also in imprisonment. The Lord uses even the experience of imprisonment. Most of the epistles of the New Testament were written from prisons. Daniel and Ezekiel received the prophetic revelations from God when they were under captivity. It is a tradition that prophets continue to do their ministry even in the prison.

(II Chr. 16:7-10, 18:23-26, Jer. 20:1, 2, Jer.37:21, Jer. 38:6, Matt. 14:3, 23:34)

20.5 Death punishment

The Israelites had the habit of killing God's prophets. Jesus Christ pointed out that it was a traditional practice in Israel. He revealed that this cruelty would continue in the future also. Jesus said, "Therefore, indeed, I send you prophets, wise men, and scribes: Some of them you will kill and crucify, and some of them you will scourge in your synagogues and persecute from city to city." "O Jerusalem, Jerusalem, the one who kills the prophets and stones those who are sent to her. How often I wanted to gather your children together as a hen gathers her brood under her wings but you were not willing!"

God rescues His prophets till the foreordained time. Elijah was threatened with murder, but he was never killed; instead, he was taken up into heaven without seeing death. During the time of tribulation, the Antichrist will murder the two prophets only after the completion of their ministry. A true prophet may be killed, but death is never a defeat for him. People may be able to kill true prophets, but they cannot destroy them. The verse, "Even the voices of the Prophets which are read every Sabbath" indicates that even after the death of the prophets God uses their words. Till the day Heaven declares the fall of the great Babylon, they will have tribulation. Till the number of martyrs is completed, killing of prophets will also continue.

(Matt. 23:31-34, Luke 13:34, Acts 13:27, I Kings. 23:16-18)

CHAPTER 21

The Prophet
and God's Protection

"... **Do My prophets no harm**" Ps. 105:15

As prophetic ministry is more dangerous than other ministries, God provides special protection for prophets. Till the appointed time, God protects them.

21.1 God's direct protection

"They will fight against you, but they shall not prevail against you. For I am with you, to deliver you" (Jer. 1:19)

It is very clear that God Himself protected Daniel in the lion's den. God does not send His prophets alone by themselves. **He goes along with them to deliver them**. God is a shield to His prophets. The hand of the Lord is upon them. Once Jehoiakim commanded his son and others to seize Jeremiah the prophet and Baruch the scribe but the Lord hid them. It was in Zarephath, in the region of Sidon that God protected Elijah for 3 years. When Jesus Christ was just a baby, the devil through Herod planned to kill Him. But the angel of the Lord directed Joseph to move to Egypt and protected Christ from the cunning devices of the enemy. When Jews took up stones to throw at Jesus, he escaped from them. On another occasion, they took him to a hilltop to throw Him down, and he disappeared.

Jeremiah declared, "But the Lord is with me as a mighty, awesome one. Therefore, my persecutors will stumble, and will not prevail. They will be greatly ashamed, for they will not prosper. Their everlasting confusion will never be forgotten."

(Dan. 6:20-24, Lk. 1:66, 4:52, 27, Jer. 36:26, Matt. 2:13, 2:14, 15, Jn. 8:59; 10:31, 7:30 Lk. 4:29, Jer. 20:11)

21.2 He saves them by giving wisdom

The king of Syria sent his man to capture Elisha. But they were struck with blindness and Elisha brought them to the king of Israel in Samaria, prepared a great for them and then sent them array. So the bands of Syrian raiders came no more into the land of Israel As God knows the enemies deceptive plans, He gives wisdom to His prophets that they might not get caught in them. Paul, who was also a prophet, escaped from many places by claiming that he was a Roman citizen. When a group of Pharisees and Sadducees had rebelled against him, he spoke about the resurrection of the dead and as that caused confusion amongst them, and he was able to escape from them.

(II Kings. 6:18-23)

21.3 The Angelic protection.

The servant of Elisha saw the mountain was full of horses and chariots of fire all around Elisha. Take note how much protection was given to a prophet. God Himself decides when and how long He should protect them through His angels. We read in the Acts of the Apostles how the angels set Peter free from the prison. It is also written in the Bible how God sent His angel against Balaam who acted against the perfect will of God. When the prophets do not stray from the way of God but fulfill all His commands the protection and ministry of the angels of God are surely given till the time set by God.

II Kings 6:17

21.4 Help through men

God used men to rescue and nourish the Lord's prophets in the days when Jezebel was killing the Lord's prophets -- Obadiah hid one hundred prophets of God in a cave and fed them with bread and water. When Jeremiah was cast into a dungeon where there was no water, Ebed Melech spoke solicitously to the king, got his permission and lifted him out of the dungeon. Till the appointed time, God gives protection to His prophets and nurtures them. It is the duty of the prophet to fulfill his ministry within the stipulated time set by God. What we have done for God is more important than how long we live.

(I Kings. 18:13, Jer. 38:7-13)

CHAPTER 22

Recognizing the true Prophets

New Testament believers should recognize true prophets and accept them. The local churches should send the true prophets out to minister in other places for the benefit of the whole Church. Generally, prophets are not accepted in their own home, town and country. It is written in the Bible about the incident where Amaziah, the priest rejected Amos. What happened to this priest who forbade prophesying? God's judgment came upon him, his wife and his children. It is clear that there would be punishment for those who reject God's true prophets.

(Act. 13:1, 2, Matt. 13:57,; 23:29,37; Mark 6:4; Lk. 4:24, Amos. 7:12-17)

22.1 Acceptance

Elders of the church have more responsibility to identify prophets and release them for ministry.

"Even if a prophet is not appointed, it is necessary to at least identify and recognize him" – Reinhard Bonke

22.2 The outcome of acceptance.

Jehoshaphat counseled, **"Believe His prophets and you shall prosper** (II Chro. 20:20). He who receives a prophet in the name of a prophet shall receive a prophet's reward (Matt. 10:41). We receive Prophetic edification. The Lord's body is being built up. We take part in the restoration of prophetic ministry.

CHAPTER 23

The Babylon and the Prophets

23.1 The trumpet sound against the Babylon

"Rejoice over her (Babylon), O heaven, and you holy apostles and prophets, for God has avenged you on her! said the angel...and in her was found the blood of prophets and saints and of all who were slain on the earth." (Rev. 18:20, Rev. 18:24)

God's purpose is to transform the Church into the Bride of the Lamb, New Jerusalem. But the deceptive plan of the enemy is to change her into Babylon, the bride of Antichrist. If we keenly observe the Church history, this truth can be clearly seen. The Church, after three hundred years of its establishment, had lost the life and turned to be a Babylonian organization. From fourth century to thirteenth century, the Church functioned as Babylon and murdered countless saints who stood zealously for the Lord's Word. Till the Roman Emperor Constantine was converted, there were no tower type church buildings. He changed the Church as a government religion, made the church buildings like the temples of pagan religions, and brought in the rites and worship pattern of other religions. As a whole, he changed the Church into a worldly religion -- contrary to the pattern of the Church established by the Lord. This is called the Dark Age in the history of the Church. Jesus Christ, the Royal Lion of Judah, separated a man (Martin Luther) from Babylon and started to rebuild his Church.

The Babylonism has crept into the universal body of Christ. Although the Lord has separated the Church from the Babylon a few centuries back, the Church keeps loving Babylon. Babylon's method of leadership and Babylon's doctrines have got into the Church and bewitched her. God's workers embrace and cherish Babylonian titles. There is a great acceptance today to Babylon's ostentatious festivals. They got used to accept such festivals and celebrating them in Babylonian style. There was a time, in which forgiveness of sin was sold through tickets in the Babylonian church. In the same way, today many people follow the Babylonian commercial methods -- selling prayers, spiritual gifts, prayer-oil, and power handkerchiefs. Even the church leaders do not hesitate to follow the Babylonian dress code. It is a very painful thing that they change the spiritual churches into institutions following the Babylonian system. She causes the servants of God to consider the size of the congregation rather than its spirituality. She hides filthiness in a golden cup which is a religious sanctimonious.

Making a name for one's own self and seeking self praise rather than doing God's will are the ultimate objects of those who follow Babylon. Obviously, Babylon is built on self- centeredness, by self-strength, and for self- glory. At the place called Babel, people began to build a high tower to make a name for them. She entices all nations by her sorcery. How good it will be if God shows us the Babylon that has crept in and got rooted in the churches! Perhaps, God is against the system of Babylon. **True prophets never compromise with her and they won't drink what she offers them through a golden cup.** In the last days, she will be raised up by the Antichrist. Babylon that has kept growing for many centuries will reach its fullness in the days of Antichrist and will excel in religion, economy and politics. True Prophets are able to rightly recognize the Babylon and to stand against her characteristics that are seen in today's Church.

"On her forehead a name was written, "Mystery, Babylon the great, the mother of harlots and of the abominations of the earth."

And I saw a woman, drunk with the blood of the saints and with the blood of the martyrs of Jesus. And when I saw her I marveled with great amazement." Rev. 17:5, 6

Prophets warn about the Babylon seen within God's people; they challenge them to come out of Babylon. They cry, **"Come out of her, my people lest you share in her sins and lest you receive of her plagues." "Up Zion! Escape, you who dwell with the daughter of Babylon."**

God is calling us to come out of Babylon and to put on the nature of Christ to live a victorious life. As Prophets do not compromise with Babylon but stand against her, they are subject to the attacks of Babylon. She is drunk with the blood of the saints and the blood of the martyrs of Jesus. The apostles and prophets are much affected and afflicted by Babylon. God will bring judgment on her for murdering the apostles and prophets. Till the day of Babylon's judgment, prophets will be exposing her characteristics to the Body of Christ.

(Joel 1:4, Matt. 16:18, Joel 2:25, Gen. 11:4, Rev. 17:4,18:23, 18:4, 17:6, 18:20, Zech 2:7)

23.2 Reforming Jeremiah

"See, I have this day set you over the nations and over the kingdoms to root out and to pull down, to destroy and to throw down, to build and to plant" (Jer. 1:10)

Jeremiahs are needed to destroy the Babylon which is being built inside the Body of Christ. When Jesus saw the temple being turned into a den of thieves, the zeal of the Lord consumed Him. He rose up in wrath against the trading going on in the temple. Will He keep quiet while seeing the Babylon in the present day Church?

The system of Babylon entered into the churches as a seed and has grown up today as a huge tree. Jesus said, **"Every plant which My heavenly Father has not planted**

will be uprooted." Likewise, the day is coming soon to uproot the Babylonian system from His glorious church. God wishes to pull out, demolish, destroy and exterminate Babylon that has been built up. For the weapons of our warfare are not carnal but mighty in God for pulling down strongholds, casting down arguments and every high thing that exalts itself against the knowledge of God, bringing every thought into captivity to the obedience of Christ. According to this word the Babylonian systems will be demolished. The Church is the living Body of Christ while the Babylon remains as a lifeless religion.

Babylon is the enemy's kingdom. Wherever the Babylon system is found, there is room for the enemy's rule. The system of Babylon found in the Church should be overthrown. First, the works of uprooting, demolishing, destroying and overturning should be done before building and planting could be done. Let us keep in mind the prophecy uttered by Zechariah during the days when the rebuilding of the temple was taken up. **"Who are you, O Great Mountain? Before Zerubbabel you shall become a plain."** The Tabernacle and the temple of Jerusalem were built according to the model in the heart of God. In the same way, the New Testament temple is also being built up in the model God already has in His heart. **"Let each one take heed how he builds on it... Each one's work will become manifest."** During the days of Babylonian captivity, the walls of Jerusalem were broken down and its gates were burned with fire. Mount Zion was desolate with foxes walking about on it. The condition of today's temple is similar. However, God's promise is that he would again do the work of restoration in the Church.

"And they shall rebuild old ruins. They shall raise up the former desolations and they shall repair the ruined cities, the desolation of many generations."

Isaiah 61:4."Those from among you shall build the old waste places; you shall raise up the foundations of many generations; and you shall be called the Repairer of Breach, the Restorer of streets to dwell in." Isaiah 58:12

God is transforming His Church into a glorious Church, not having spot or wrinkle or any such thing, but that it should be holy and without blemish. He will completely remove all the characteristics of the Babylon seen in it. As He brought out the matter of the Babylonian garment which Achan had hidden, even so the day is near when He will expose through His prophets the Babylonian characteristics.

Where are the men like Jeremiah to demolish the Babylon and build up the Lord's Church?

(John 2:14-17, Matt.15:13, II Cor.10:4, 5, Jer.50:14, 15, 15:6-64, Isa. 14:4-15, Zech. 4:7, I Cor.3:10, 13, Neh.1:3, Lam. 5:18, Eph. 5:27)

CHAPTER 24

Prophetic Ministry and the End Time Revival

One of the most common truths we can observe from the history of the Church is that God sends His Word and revives His people. Till now, there have been revivals here and there in some countries -- mostly, God used a specific man in each country. In the past, God sent revivals to the Church through many men like John Wesley, Jonathan Edwards, Charles Finney and Spurgeon. The move of the Holy Spirit took place only in a particular region of this world. But, the End Time Revival is not confined to any particular place or country -- it belongs to the whole Church of Christ. Forthcoming revival will cause the Church to restore everything that she had lost in the past centuries. We are waiting for the Great move – the end-time move -- of the Spirit of God. God is preparing the prophetic ministry in these days for the end-time – world-wide -- Revival. The vision of the valley of bones which Ezekiel saw is a shadow of the end time revival. Let us seek the help of the Holy Spirit to understand this vision in a new dimension.

24.1 The Valley of Dry Bones

What does the valley of dry bones signify?

"The hand of the Lord came upon me and brought me out in the Spirit of the Lord, and set me down in the midst of the valley; and it was full of bones. Then He caused me to pass by them all around, and behold, there were many in the open valley; and indeed they were very dry." (Ezek 37:1, 2)

Through this vision, God showed and explained Ezekiel the true inner spiritual condition of His people. In the valley of dry bones, only the lifeless -- very dry – motionless -- and hopeless bones were seen. God gave this vision when the people of Israel were in a hopeless state under Babylonian captivity. He gathered the bones together and made them into a mighty army. This demonstration gave hope that He would gather the Israelites again in their own country. Accordingly, it happened so. At the same time, the next stage of fulfillment would be in the last days. The Israelites -- scattered in many countries would again be gathered together in their own country. In 1948, the country of Israel was again formed; Jews who were scattered all over the world for many centuries were again gathered together. This is the proof that God will fulfill His prophecy completely. The vision that Ezekiel saw indicates the condition of Israel as well as the Church. What God has done literally for Israel, He does them spiritually to the Church. The Israel was the shadow of the New Testament Church and in God's plan, the Church is the ultimate reality.

The Israelites are the earthly descendants of Abraham like the sands on the sea shore while the believers in the New Testament Church are the spiritual descendants of Abraham like the stars of the heaven. That is why the Bible explains that Abraham is the father of the Israelites as well as of the Church. God will fulfill Ezekiel's vision for Israel literally and He will fulfill that vision for the Church spiritually. The valley of the dry bones reveals us that the hopeless condition of today's Church which lacks the flow of life and got divided in many aspects. All that happened to Israel are examples; they are written to give us warning as we are in the end times of the world. Ultimately, God showed in a vision to Ezekiel what He would do with His New Testament Church in the end times.

(I Cor. 15:19, 1 Cor. 1:12, 10:11)

24.2 The Church seen in the valley of bones.

What is the connection between the Church and the valley of bones?

When God revealed the mystery of the church of Laodicea to John, truly he might have been shocked. Listen carefully to what the Laodicean church declared about its spiritual condition, "I am rich and have become wealthy and have need of nothing." This was a wrong positive confession. Christ listened to their declaration keenly. But, He knew exactly what their spiritual condition was. Time and again, in some parts of the world, there's a revival going on; but, the revival of the universal Church is yet to come. The standard of the Church has gone down in many aspects: cross-less Christ in being preached, and there is no one bothers to see the power of the evil spirits operating in the name of the power of the Holy Spirit. People's desire is blessings -- without suffering. There's a grand welcome to a gospel message that does not include repentance. Many people accept Christianity while only a few become Disciples of Christ. At this time of crisis, most people – neglecting the judgment of God – choose to use the word of God to gain success and prosperity in this earthly life. They forget the warning of the Scripture, "If in this life only we have hope in Christ, we are of all men the most pitiable".

People as well as preachers desire a life that is centered on self-will rather than a life centered on God's will. They prefer a life of pleasure to a life of holiness. Samson was not aware of the departure of God's Spirit from him. Similarly, Laodicean church was insensitive. When Christ was standing outside the church and was knocking at the door, they said, "I am rich, have become wealthy, and have need of nothing". Indeed, they have lost the spiritual sensitivity to realize that they were poor and naked. Today's Church, being conformed to the world, seems to be salt without flavor. We live with a false satisfaction thinking that all is well. What is the true condition of today's Church?

Each day new denominations continue to blossom. People come out of existing denominations and form a new denomination or groups or sects. We have non-denominational denominations too. They think that only their denomination or group or sect is the whole body of Christ. A local church is only a part of the great universal body of Christ. There is only one Body -- one Universal Church. This sectarianism began in the first century itself and it is multiplied too much now. In the Corinthian church there were divisions and they claimed, **"I am of Paul, or I am of Apollos, or I am of Cephas, or I am of Christ".** We are unable to say that we belong to Christ. Is Christ divided? Paul, repeatedly, emphasize that the Body of Christ is only one with many members.

In Ephesians Chapter 4:4-6, Apostle Paul insists the oneness of the Church:

*For by one Spirit we were all baptized into **one body**-whether Jews or Greeks, whether slaves or free and have all been made to drink into **one Spirit**. There is **one body** and **one Spirit** just as you were called in **one hope** of your calling, **one Lord**, **one faith**, **one baptism**, **one God** and **Father of all**, who is above all and through all and in you all.*

We can say that today's Church has forgotten the place, where God has brought the believers into. Truly, we've come to the general assembly and the Church of the firstborn who are registered in heaven. Eventually, God's ultimate plan is to make Christ's Church in this world as one body, one city, one mansion, one temple, one house, one flock, and one farm. Christ promised, "On this rock, I will build My Church". He is building one worldwide Church on Himself. Teachings and spiritual experiences have created many divisions in the Church. He builds His own Church on Himself -- not on any other foundation. The Church is not an organization; but**, it is a living organism**. Practically speaking, we are again and again building institutions. Some people get hold of a kind of teachings and become doctinians while others get hold of gifts and slide away. Some people think that the spiritual life alone is enough and stand aloof. The truth is that we need all of them. **This is His plan that we all should grow corporately in all things in Christ the Head**. All born again believers are members of the Church of Christ. **When all of us, who are separated from one another, are gathered together as ONE ARMY and stand together on the earth, we can say we have a REVIVAL.**

Leonard Ravenhill writes very indefatigably in the editorial of his book, *"Revival in God's way"* about the condition of today's Church which is still in the valley of dry bones. A revival is necessary for all of us to come to **the unity of the faith** and **the knowledge of the Son of God, to a perfect man**, to the measure of **the stature of the fullness of Christ.** There will be onness in the whole Church, according to Christ's prayer, **"That they all may be one, as You, Father, (are) in Me, and I in You; that they also may be one in us"**

(Rev.3:17-20, 1Cor 1:12, Romans 12:5, I Cor 12:12, 13, Heb 12:22, 23, Eph. 4:13, John. 17:21, Matt 16:18)

24.3 The Prophet sent to the dry bones

Again He said to me, "Prophesy to these bones, and say to them, O dry bones, hear the word of the LORD!" (Ezek 37:1-4)

God led Ezekiel to see Israel in the valley of dry bones. Yes, seeing God's people according to God's perspective is the first step in prophetic ministry. God's dimension is completely different from human. John also saw the churches when he was in Spirit. John was in the Spirit on the Lord's Day which is relevant to the experience of Ezekiel. God sent Ezekiel to the valley of dry bones. We need prophets like Ezekiel to see today's valley of dry bones. God's command was to prophesy to the very dry bones that they should hear the Word of the Lord. Remember that there is no life in the bones and they do not have the ability to hear. How then can a dry bone hear anyone's voice? Talking to dry bones is completely contrary to the human intelligence. It is only through faith we can speak to the dry bones. It was because Joseph had the faith that after 430 years of slavery, God would visit the Israelites and that they would be set free to leave Egypt and accordingly he had given instruction about his bones. Though we have the revelation of what God is going to do, we need faith and obedience to make those things known. Ezekiel, as an obedient prophet, prophesied as he was COMMANDED. If the end-time revival has to take place in the Church, obedient prophets like Ezekiel are needed. **You too can be one of the prophets that God is looking for.**

As he prophesied, there was a noise which shows the move of the Holy Spirit. On the day of Pentecost suddenly there was a sound from heaven as a rushing mighty wind as the Holy Spirit was poured out upon them. We are waiting for the great move of the Holy Spirit. There is going to be a loud noise in the present valley of dry bones too. And suddenly a rattling; and the bones came together, bone to bone. Each bone began to move! They went back to the original and former places joining together with other bones. This is the work of the Spirit of God. He joins the bones to their own original places. **"Not by might nor by power, but by My SPIRIT" says the Lord.** This will also happen in the Church according to God's word. No one can stand against the move of the spirit because it is not organized by any man. According to God's promise, there's going to be a great shaking in the Church before he shakes the heavens.

Because Ezekiel prophesied to the bones, they came together -- bone to bone -- and sinews and flesh and skin came upon them and covered them. This is totally an experience of a new creation. He says, **"Behold, I make all things new."** He will also make all things new in the Church. The Heavenly Jerusalem is going to be changed into the New Jerusalem. It is the time of revival, restoration, and reformation. **The day is near when the fivefold ministry is again going to be operative in the churches.**

(Ez. 37:11, Rev1:10; Eze.37:1, Ezek.37:4, Ezek 37:7, Ezek 37:7, Acts. 2:2, Ezek 37:7, Zech. 4:6, Ezek 37:8, Heb. 12:26, Rev. 21:5, Heb.12: 22; Rev. 21:2)

24.4 A New Army formed out of dry bones

What happened next in the valley of bones?

"So I prophesied as He commanded me, and breath came into them, and they lived, and stood upon their feet, an exceedingly great army." (Ezek 37:10)

What was the condition of the church in Sardis? "… **I know your works, that you have a name you that you are alive, but you are dead."** When God blows His breath of life into the Church, a new life is created. The blowing of the Holy Spirit on the Church afresh like a wind is a revival -- the move of the fresh breath of God upon the Church-- will cause her to come out of the dead experiences. It is sure that when new life penetrates through the whole Body of Christ, the worldwide Church will receive a new enthusiasm. It was mandatory for Ezekiel to speak the word of God before the life entered into the dry bones. Before God sends revival inside the Church, some people have to speak God's living word -- as prophecy.

"They stood upon their feet, an exceedingly great army". Life alone is not sufficient to stand by the feet, but they also need the strength to stand as they received life after many years. **The Holy Spirit is not only life-giving Spirit but also the power giving Spirit.** Jesus promised, **"You shall receive power when the Holy Spirit has come upon you."** The Holy Spirit turns the dry bones into a great army. God has not just changed the numerous bones into a group of people; instead, he has made them into a great army. Surely, **God is raising up an ARMY.** In this hopeless situation, deceptive doctrines and signs are attracting the people of God and the divisions are increasing day by day; God wants an army to accomplish His will on the earth and demolish the powers of darkness. This army is none other than the army of the Lord; such an army existed never before in the history. In the last days, they shall run as horsemen, they shall run like mighty men, and the Lord is going to utter his voice before his army. And Daniel prophesied that the people who know their God should become strong and do exploits.

God is making the Church as a bride as well as an army. They that are with Him in the war are called, chosen, and faithful. **The need of this hour is not another denomination -- but A NEW ARMY.** Before the Church marches out from the valley of dry bones, it will be transformed into a new army.

"Who is she who looks forth as the morning, fair as the moon, clear as the sun, and awesome as an army with banners?"(Songs of Solomon 6:10)

(Eph. 5:14 Rev. 3:1 Ezek. 37:10, Rom. 8:2, Acts. 1:8, Joel 2:11, Joel 2:1-11, Dan. 11:32, Rev. 17:14; 19:14)

24.5 The New Army and the Temple of the Lord.

At the end days, God will use an army to renew and build His church. When the people of Israel were captives, he compared their condition to dry bones. According to the prophecy of Jeremiah, after the set time, God raised an army for Himself. They moved out from Babylon to Jerusalem and rebuilt the city and the temple. Nehemiah, Zerubbabel, Joshua, Zechariah, Ezra, and Haggai had important roles to play in that army. The zealous people did the construction work with one hand while holding a weapon in another hand. Irrespective of oppositions, they repaired and built the temple. Zechariah prophesied about the restoration of the New Testament temple: **Behold, the Man whose name is the BRANCH. He shall build the temple of the Lord.** This verse talks about the visitation of God to restore his temple in the last days.

The Lord will build up Zion before his glorious appearance. While rebuilding the temple he will fill his prophets with anointing and use them. Zechariah's vision reveals that, in the last days, God will send His Spirit into the churches through his prophetic words. This vision was given when the re-building work of Jerusalem and the temple was taken up. Zechariah and Haggai functioned as prophets in the team involved in the ministry of restoration. Two olive trees were symbols of the prophetic ministry of those days. To affirm this thought, there was another vision given to John in the book of Revelation. John writes that there are the two lampstands standing before God and the two lamps represents two prophets who will prophesy for 1260 days during the period of Antichrist. It is evident that the olive trees are the symbol of prophetic ministry and the lamp stand are the symbol of witnessing.

The end time prophetic team is going to function as olive trees. When the anointed ones speak the words, the life and power will flow abundantly. **We should understand that the gold pipes denote God's holy words, the golden lampstand denotes the Church, the golden olive oil denotes the anointing, and the olive trees denote the team of prophets who stands before God.**

In these days, God is sanctifying and maturing the olive trees that stand in His presence to get ready for His end time revival. God is filling them with His anointing. At the right time, through his holy prophetic words that they are going to speak the anointing of life and power will gush forth. Eventually, **this fresh oil of the anointing will cause a revival in the lampstand -- the Church of Christ -- and it will stand on the earth as a glorious witness for Christ.** Only those who have received the anointing and are standing before the Lord will have a part in this kind of ministry. When the temple in Jerusalem was burnt, God showed a new temple to Ezekiel. The model of the temple and its measurements were totally different from the former temple. The temple that the Lord showed Ezekiel was actually the model for the New Testament Church which would exist in the last days.

We find the water flowing from under the threshold of the temple toward the east and wherever the river goes there's an impartation of life. There will be a great multitude of fish, there will be healing, there will be prosperity of trees used for food, and there will fruit-bearing at regular interval. Compare these verses with the promise given by the Lord Jesus Christ, "Out of his heart will flow rivers of living water."

From God's renewed – cleansed -- end time temple, rivers of living water will flow abundantly. This river indicates the Holy Spirit. God's glory will descend upon the end- time Church. When Moses completed the tabernacle of meeting, the glory of the Lord filled the tabernacle. In the same way, when Solomon completed the temple the glory of the Lord came down,and the priests couldn't enter the house of the Lord. If God's glory descended on the tabernacle of Moses and the Jerusalem temple which were the shadow of the Church, how much more it's certain that the glory of the Lord would descend upon the New Testament Church on its completion?

"The glory of this latter temple shall be greater than the former" says the Lord of hosts.

Let the anointed ones rise up and prophesy so that dry bones shall become alive.

(Neh. 4:16, 17, Zech. 6:12, 13, Ps. 102:16, Zech. 4:1-3, 4:12,14, Rev. 11:3, 10, 11:4, Ez. 40 to 45, 47:1, 47:9, 12, John 7:38, Ezek. 47:1-5, Ex. 40:34,35, I Chr.28: 19; II Chr. 3:1, Haggai 2:9)

CHAPTER 25

Prepare for the End Time Prophetic move

25.1 The former and the latter Rain

Pray for the latter rain. (Zech 10:1)

God says through Zechariah to ask for the latter rain in the last days, and the Holy Spirit will manifest His power in an extraordinary way. This latter rain is specially granted to prosper the prophetic ministry. John the Baptist was the forerunner of Jesus and testified that Christ Jesus is the Lamb of God. In the same way, the prophets and ministers who receive the prophetic anointing will have a major part in the ministry of preparing the people of God for the second coming of Jesus Christ and they will also testify that Jesus Christ is the Messiah. God has commanded the New Testament Church also to pray for the latter rain. God expects us to seek him with a great burden and turn to Him in order to experience the outpouring of the Holy Spirit. Elijah prayed, and the rain came.

We've to lament like Jeremiah, "**Turn us unto Thee Oh Lord, then shall we be turned; renew our days as of old days**". We should seek the Lord as it is said in Joel, "**Turn to Me with all your heart, with fasting with weeping, and with mourning. So rend your heart and not your garments. Return to the Lord your God**." We should call the people to gather together to pray. "**Blow the trumpet in Zion. Consecrate a fast. Call a sacred assembly. Gather the people. Sanctify the congregation**".

Note the call given by Joel with a great sense of seriousness to gather the people together to pray for the latter rain.

"Assemble the Elders, Gather the children and nursing babes. Let the bridegroom go out from his chamber, and the bride from her dressing room. Let the priests, who minister to the Lord, weep between the porch and the altar." (Joel. 2:16, 17)

What will happen when God's people gather together to pray with fasting and mourning? Equivocally, God will answer His people and will send both **the former and the latter rain together.** Before doing the wonders in the heavens and on the earth, He will send the great rain of the Spiri on His Church. He will fulfill His promise and there shall be showers of blessings. He promised us, *"In the last days I will pour out My Spirit on all flesh. Your sons and daughters will prophesy; And also on my* *menservants and on my maidservants, I will pour out My Spirit in those days.... they shall prophesy".* There shall be streams in the desert, parched ground shall become a pool, and the thirsty land shall become springs of water. When God planted the Church on this earth He sent the former rain, and before harvesting his Church from this earth He will send the latter rain. He waits for the precious fruit of the earth patiently until it receives the early and the latter rain.

Indeed, God is raising people who shall pray for the latter rain. According to the promise of God, Joel 2:23, he poured out the former rain upon the Church in the first century, and in these days he is going to pour out a two-fold rain -- t**he former and the latter rain**. The loud noise of heavy rain is going to be heard. Following the latter rain, the prophetic ministry will undergo a rapid growth. Since the prophets and prophesying believers continue to prophesy over the Church, an army will rise up to shake the world. The Church will restore all that it has lost. Then, God will bring His Church into perfection and make her as His beloved bride. **God is raising the end-time believers as a prophetic generation.** Let us be prepared for the prophetic move and let us prepare others too. Let us cry in God's presence with burden and longing for revival. Let the fire of revival spread in every Nation.

This is the time for the latter rain; now is the time for the prophetic ministry.

"The Lord God has spoken! Who can but prophesy?"

(Amos 3:8, Joel 2:12 -16, Joel. 2:19, 2:23, 28-30, Ezek 34:26, Acts 2:17-18, Isa 35:6, 7, James 5:7, 18, *Zech 10:1, Heb 6:3, Matt 24:14, Act 18:5)*

Printed in the United States
By Bookmasters